HE'S A LIL' QUIRKY

An Unexpected Journey into Autism Spectrum Disorder

JON LOCKE

CLAY BRIDGES
PRESS

He's a Lil' Quirky
An Unexpected Journey into Autism Spectrum Disorder

Copyright © 2019 by Jon Locke

Published by Clay Bridges Press in Houston, TX

eISBN-10: 1-63296-391-4 | eISBN-13: 978-1-63296-391-8
ISBN-10: 1-63296-351-5 | ISBN-13: 978-1-63296-351-2

Scripture quotations are taken from the Holy Bible, New International Version®, NIV®. Copyright © 1973, 1978, 1984, 2011 by Biblica, Inc.™ Used by permission of Zondervan. All rights reserved worldwide. www.zondervan.com The "NIV" and "New International Version" are trademarks registered in the United States Patent and Trademark Office by Biblica, Inc.™

Special Sales: Most Clay Bridges Press titles are available in special quantity discounts. Custom imprinting or excerpting can also be done to fit special needs. Contact Clay Bridges Press at info@claybridgespress.com.

"*He's a Lil' Quirky* is an honest, heartfelt look at the face of autism. It offers real situations faced by a real family. Most importantly, this book offers hope and love throughout the journey. I encourage anyone traveling down the road with someone with autism to read this book. It is refreshing and insightful, and I will definitely have it on my shelf as I work with students and parents."

—**Resha Tanner,**
EdM in Special Education with
Educational Diagnostician Certification

"Jon's book will open your eyes and break open your heart with a heartwarming and informative story of his family's journey with autism. If autism has touched your life or you are looking for more knowledge about this topic, this book needs to be on your nightstand. It's fantastic and highly recommended."

—**Nik Tebbe Writer,**
Grief Support Specialist

"As a professional therapist who has worked with individuals and families dealing with a wide array of mental health and developmental concerns, I am honored to have been asked to read and review Jon's personal story regarding autism and its impact on a family. I was deeply touched by the authenticity and raw description of this prevalent and all too often misunderstood 'disorder.' I found myself laughing and in tears, all within the same few pages. Thank you for such a heartfelt, journalistic window view into such a complex and confusing reality called autism."

—**Abby Wirick,**
LMHC and NCC

"As a licensed professional counselor, I admire your ability to share your personal experiences with the world. I found your recollections of your struggles will help individuals and families facing similar struggles realize that they aren't alone and also inspire hope within them. Your testimony is powerful, and I appreciate how you make the reader feel close to you by inviting them to be your friend."

—**Bridget Kennedy,**
LPC, LCDC

I dedicate this book to my beautiful wife and best friend, Michele. You have sacrificed so much, even to the point of sacrificing your health for our family. There is no one I would rather be on this journey with than you; you are my everything.

I also dedicate this book to my children, Alana, Greyson, Keegan, Ian, and Kai, and to my two grandsons, Kamron and Atlas.

TABLE OF CONTENTS

SPECIAL THANKS

A very special thank you goes to my parents, Donald and Judy Locke, who have done so much for me all my life. To my brother, Don, who is and has been one of my biggest supporters. And to my sister, Mary, who consoled me after a particularly hard ministry experience by saying that "some of the best examples are on how not to do things."

I would also like to thank:
Delores Stout
Tammy Mcqurter
Rosemary Groover
Gwen Lowe
Mike and Kim Buish
Carol and Bill Bauman
Ray and Kathy Carter
Brittany Armlin
Betty Acheson
Laura Glasser
Florence Moyle
Aimee J LaFontaine
Charlene K. Morris
Michael Overstreet
Irene Isenberger
Mark Jones
Jenna Teal
Myriam Olivier

FOREWORD

As a therapist, I want to provide the people I serve with resources, practical solutions, and a whole lot of hope when they come to me for help. This book provides that hope and some practical solutions to many situations families may have to face. Jon tells of his family's struggles throughout their journey to help his son cope with his autism spectrum diagnosis as it paralleled his own story. He worked as an investigator for Child Protective Services and understands many systems families have to navigate when they are dealing with a mental health issue. His testimony is one that can inspire others as they attempt to navigate these systems themselves.

It is often very difficult for families to realize that they are not alone, and that they can make it through to the light at the end of this journey. This book can serve as a guide to help ignite the flame of hope within families who have similar struggles. Having a mental health issue is not the end of their world, as Jon says: "Do not give them or let them use their diagnoses as a crutch!"

There is still a stigma associated with mental health diagnoses in our society and it takes bravery from people like Jon to come forward and openly discuss these issues to stamp out this stigma. As a society, we need to offer acceptance to individuals who are suffering with a mental health diagnosis and encourage them that they can accomplish their dreams just like any other person can.

—Donna Daigle-Thomas, LPC, LCDC

INTRODUCTION

In various forms, this book has been in the making for many years, but due to self-doubt and low self-esteem, it never came to fruition until now. Originally, this book was supposed to be titled *They Call Me Job*, but things happen. If I had used that title, I realized that people reading the book without prior knowledge of the Bible or the reference might miss the meaning and pronunciation. Regardless of the title of the book, you will see the connection to the events in my life and why my friends and even my phone autocorrects and calls me Job! I first want to clarify that in no way am I or my friends saying that I am a righteous man like the biblical Job; I try but the Lord and especially my wife and kids know that I fall short on a daily basis.

As I mentioned above, the idea of this book has changed and morphed in my mind many times. It wasn't until early 2018 that I received the final vision for the book. It will not take you long to see the connection between the biblical Job and myself or why my nonbeliever friends call me the "unluckiest person" on the face of the planet. I cannot tell you how many times I've heard the phrase, "Jon if you didn't have bad luck, you wouldn't have any luck at all." But don't worry, this book won't be all boohooing and heaviness; there are light moments as well. I wasn't voted class clown seven years in a row for nothing! My mom still has anxiety attacks whenever she hears the words *school award ceremony*!

In all seriousness, we will be looking at the darker side of autism and the effects that it has on the individual, their family, and all the lives that they touch. This will be an authentic, honest look into our lives—the good, the bad, and the real ugly. I am sharing our story to help others. I hope that this book offers comfort and serves as a resource for a parent whose child is on the spectrum and may be struggling. This book can be a resource for a family facing an autism diagnosis or a family whose child is having difficulty but has not yet been diagnosed. Hopefully, you will find answers to some of your questions that point you in the right direction. For some, like me, you may have lived your whole life wondering why you were different. You might not look different physically, but on the inside, you always knew you were very different from the other people around you. What can make the situation worse is that this inner struggle can bring on depression and anxiety, which can be intensified because the person does not know how to communicate what is happening. Sadly, this struggle brought on severe depression and anxiety for me. Does this sound familiar? I knew I was not alone. If any of this is familiar, then this book is for you.

Before we get into my story, let's define our terminology. What is autism? Autism is known as a spectrum disorder. It is a condition related to the brain development that impacts how a person perceives and socializes with others, causing problems in social interaction and communication, such as not making eye contact or lacking facial expressions. The disorder may be characterized by limited and repetitive patterns of behavior such as rocking back and forth, spinning, or hand flapping. The term *spectrum* in autism spectrum disorder refers to the wide range of symptoms and severity, which can range from high functioning to nonverbal behavior.

Autism spectrum disorder includes conditions that were previously considered separate such as autism, Asperger syndrome, childhood disintegrative disorder, and an unspecified form of pervasive developmental disorder. Some people still use the term *Asperger syndrome*, which is generally thought to be at the mild end of autism spectrum disorder.

Autism spectrum disorder usually begins in early childhood and eventually affects how the person functions in society. Individuals who have autism spectrum disorder can expect symptoms to be manifested socially, in school and at work. Often infants show symptoms of autism within the first year. A few children appear to develop normally in the first year and then go through

Introduction

a period of regression between 18 and 24 months of age when they develop characteristics of autism. While there is no cure for autism and autism spectrum disorder, intensive, early treatment can make a big difference in children's lives.

The sad truth about autism and autism spectrum disorder is that depression is a very common side effect. All too often, depression in autistic children goes unnoticed and undiagnosed because autism is a developmental disorder that affects communication and behavior. Such a missed diagnosis can be harmful and detrimental to the individual. In the past five years, research has revealed alarming rates of suicide ideations and suicide attempts by individuals with autism. Think about how many individuals have suffered silently or lost their lives because the connection between autism and suicide ideations was not understood until recently.

My wife and I pray that this book finds you well, and we hope that, by reading this book, you will find the answers, hope, and relief you need.

CHAPTER 1

WHERE DO WE BEGIN?

The road has been long and hard; I'm not going to lie. Sometimes, I wonder how we have made it this far to be honest. The only answer I have is that God is watching out for us. It might be hard to comprehend that, but someone truly had a hand in watching over us. That's not to say that we haven't lost a lot, because we have. Once you read our story, some of you might even ask, "How can you say that God was watching out for you after all that has happened to you and your family?" Trust me; there were times that I was screaming and cursing God and daring Him to take my life because I thought I couldn't take it anymore. This deep sense of frustration happened a lot, sometimes even daily.

So, before we get too much further into my story, let me introduce my family. My wife, Michele, and I have been married going on 22 years. She is my best friend and the rock in our family. You will learn more about her later as I devote chapters to different members of our family. We have five beautiful children and a grandson who is a little rock star. Our children range in age from 5 to 22. Sadly, our 22-year-old daughter, Alana, chooses not to have a relationship with us. Our 20-year-old son, Greyson, lives in Florida since he didn't want to make the trek with us when we moved to Texas for what we call our "fresh new start." So, in our house we have our 11-year old son, Keegan, 9-year-old son, Ian, and 5-year-old son, Kai. We also have our former son-in-law, Juan, as well as our 3-year-old grandson, Kamron.

Yes, we will get to the backstory shortly. Be patient. My parents also live with us. We have a full house, but we wouldn't have it any other way. Oh! How could I forget our fur babies? Obi is our "senior" dog as my wife calls him. He was a rescue dog we got from the Navajo Reservation in Arizona when I was a youth pastor in Page, Arizona. Oreo is our little black-and-white cat who thinks she is a dog. She loves to chase people through the house and likes to have people watch her eat. It's very odd but true. Lastly, we have Po, a giant, rambunctious puppy that is a mix of Great Pyrenees and St. Bernard; he is already nearing 100 pounds, and he is a handful. The kids named him Po because as a baby he looked like a panda. So, after the movie *Kung Fu Panda*, Po seemed like the perfect name for him, not to mention how clumsy he is.

We are a homeschool family—no, not like the one featured in Tim Hawkins's song "A Homeschool Family," but we love the idea of being able to teach our kids what we want. Okay, I'm lying; we wish we could have sent our kids to school, public or private or any kind of school, but we did not feel that we could do so early on. We homeschooled our two older children for a time, but that was more for external reasons than for behavioral reasons or because of a belief system. Though, looking back, I must say that Greyson displayed some signs that we now recognize as an indication that he was possibly on the spectrum (as hindsight is always 20/20).

Initially, we chose to homeschool because our daughter was acting and modeling at the time and became so busy that the school administrators told us that Alana's excessive absences were causing her to fall behind. We did our due diligence and checked out the laws and found out that it was easy to switch to homeschooling in Florida, which I thought was really scary. I assumed that because I had a college degree and Michele was working toward her degree, our kids would be fine if we homeschooled. However, I took a dim view of allowing parents who had less education to homeschool their kids. It was just my ignorance and stereotyping, but I learned quickly that these parents and curriculums are amazing! They work together, building networks to help one another. It was so beautiful to see. I truly had to eat crow for sure. If, for example, you weren't good in math, you could reach out to another parent within your homeschool group who could teach math, and vice versa with another subject. The same strategy applied to physical education and field trips. It's such an amazing thing for the children and for the parents. I can remember all the times Michele would cry in frustration when we first started homeschooling because she felt she was all alone. Then, when we joined the parent groups, she found out that she wasn't alone, and to this day, we still have lasting friendships formed through our parent network.

By 2006, Alana was doing a lot of modeling near where we lived in Florida and some acting in other parts of the Southeast, which got her recognized by a well-known agent in Atlanta. Once that connection was made, things seemed to really take off. Alana did commercials, print work, and two major motion pictures through her agent's referral to an agent in Hollywood. During this time, I was the one who traveled with Alana as I was on disability due to problems with my back. Michele stayed home with Greyson and also worked as a hairstylist. It was a very exciting time, but it was also a very destructive time for our family. Greyson also did some acting and modeling; his biggest role was an appearance on an autopsy show on the Discovery Channel. He would have preferred to be in the background, but he didn't mind getting the paychecks.

Why are we here in Texas—the land of my birth? Oh boy, this is probably one of the craziest stories you will ever hear, but it is all 100 percent true. Okay, we are here because after 2016, Michele finally said, "If you want to move back to Texas, we can go." This was huge for me! Michele does not like being hot, and folks, Texas gets hot! In fact, as I write this chapter, it's going to be 106 degrees today; as I like to say, "But it's a dry heat." But at 106, dry or wet, it's hot!

The Trials of 2016 Marked a Turning Point in Our Journey

You may be wondering why 2016—what was a turning point for us? To answer that question, I have to go back to December 2015 and recall the traumatic sequence of events that led up to our move from Florida to Texas. See, I had a full beard, like a *Duck Dynasty* kind of beard. I had it because every Christmas Michele and I painted my beard and my hair white, and I dressed up as Santa Claus for kids who were in the care of Child Protective Services (CPS) or kids who were assigned as part of my workload. I brought them gifts because their families could't afford gifts, a tree, or Christmas dinner. I loved to do this because I wanted to change the perception of CPS. We were hated. We have been called the devil! So, anything that I could do to change the perception of the department, I did.

But getting back to my story: In December 2015, I noticed a spot on my face under my beard, and it started to become raised and hard as a rock. Of course, Michele wanted me to shave my beard and go to the doctor, but I was like, "Hello! I'm Santa! I cannot disappoint the kids!" So, after Christmas 2015, I shaved and yes, the spot was still there, so I reluctantly went to my primary care doctor, who referred me to a specialist. The specialist was a really nice doctor, and she initially thought it was an infected hair follicle, but she took a sample of it anyway just to calm Michele's nerves. While she was doing that, she noticed that I had other spots, and she decided to slice and dice on them as well. She called them "an outward sign of an inward problem."

To make a long story short, they did a lot of tests and found that my thyroid levels were abnormal. This led to several scans, and the results really shook Michele and me to our core. I had never had any medical problems like this, and it was just not good timing as we began to think the worst. I was sent to a surgeon for a biopsy because three nodules were found on the right side of my thyroid. The biopsy confirmed that I had the big C. For the next hour, and probably the next week, the doctor and his staff asked me if I had ever been exposed to a large amount of radiation. I was like, "What?" What we learned was that thyroid cancer is rare for men. It is still a mystery as to why and how I got it. I'm still dealing with this diagnosis by the way.

So, as I was being prepped for surgery in April 2016, the doctor explained that after they removed a portion of the thyroid, they would do a biopsy to see what type of cancer I had. I woke up, and all had gone well, especially since I woke up! The doctor informed us that they couldn't do the biopsy during the surgery because the mass was rock hard. But there was also bad news; the left side of my thyroid would have to be removed in a second surgery. He gave us two options: do it soon or wait till I heal from the first surgery. We chose to do it soon as that was also his recommendation (June 2016). We just wanted to get the growth out of me, so we could get on with the treatment to get cancer-free.

Where Do We Begin?

If having cancer wasn't bad enough, 2016 was not done with me! Some might say the worst was yet to come. As I told you earlier, I work for CPS; more specifically, I am an investigator, which means I am on the front line. Quite often, I see the abuse and neglect before law enforcement and medical professionals. Trust me when I say I have seen things that would make most people have nightmares or throw up. I have always found it odd that law enforcement officers often tell me that they couldn't do my job, which is funny because I don't think I could do theirs. Being an investigator is truly the toughest and most rewarding job I have ever done, but it takes a toll on me and my family for sure. My psychiatrist (yes, I have a psychiatrist) once told me, "Jon, doing this type of work will either be a complete and utter disaster, or it will be truly beautiful and turn out great."

Let me also self-disclose a bit more before we go on this amazing journey that is about to unfold. I am a germaphobe! I am always washing my hands and using hand sanitizer; I have a problem. But it's a good problem, I think. I will leave out all the crazy things I do or won't do or touch. I will spare you the details. In the child protection world, we get all kinds of cases, not only those involving parents physically abusing their children or sexual abuse. A lot of cases involve filthy homes. I'm not talking about, "Oh, I feel lazy today, and I'm just not going to pick up around the house."

Sometimes, the homes I visit belong to hoarders and are filled with trash. Sometimes, small children live in these filthy homes, and small children cannot self-protect. So, they are in danger in their home environment. In such cases, CPS has to go in and wear a bunch of hats for these parents. For some, it's the parent hat, the life coach hat, and the professional organizer hat because the parents do not understand that these conditions are not acceptable for small children and not healthy for them either. Oh, the stories I could tell.

I digress. I'll share an example of the kind of situation I sometimes find when CPS is called in. At one appointment, I was meeting with another provider to help a family with services because they were struggling with some things. I truly wanted to help this family. I had dedicated so much time and money to this family. I would buy cleaning products and other items for their house only to have the parents return them for other things. Their home was bad, but it wasn't "remove kids" bad yet because the kids were older, and they should have been helping their mom and dad clean. So, I showed up with the provider, and she didn't even want to sit at their kitchen table because roaches were running across it. But we had been trained to try to avoid pointing out things that would hurt people's feelings or embarrass them. I sat down and I pulled out a chair for the other provider, and she reluctantly sat down. The parents sat with us, and we began talking as I was moving roaches off my paperwork. The mom tried to act as if the roaches weren't there. I could tell that she was visibly uncomfortable and embarrassed by the condition of her home. (Quick backstory and information for you all: dirty homes and hoarding are generational, and usually a learned behavior.) Come to find out this mom came from a family that was very clean, and she had been the same way, but her husband was from a family of hoarders, and he was just flat-out lazy. So, after years of being married, she just got tired and gave up; she became just like her husband. Sadly, their children will follow in their footsteps unless something or someone intervenes in their lives.

The father made jokes about the roaches as he killed them with his bare hands. I was trying not to throw up while seeing this. Boy, did this man have the excuses, and like I said, we had been taught not to embarrass people. However, we do have to call them out sometimes. I don't want y'all to think that we didn't call them out, because trust me, I did. During this visit, we also noticed large amounts of feces on the floor and on one of the walls; to this day, I still do not know what or who was the perpetrator. I had forgotten my pen in my car, and the provider "claimed" she didn't have one either, so the mom handed me her pen and, without thinking, I took it. The thought that I had hand sanitizer in the car flashed in my mind. The presence of feces, the lack of cleanliness in the home, and the lack of progress argued for the need to remove the children from the home. I thought there was no way I could leave those two girls in this home. Just no way!

I went outside and called my supervisor and began to plead my case, but she didn't agree! I'm like, "No way am I leaving this house without these girls!" But my supervisor didn't budge, even after all that I told her and even after what the provider told her, we didn't remove the kids. The CPS system was so messed up; it was just ridiculous. But we did remove the children a week later.

Where Do We Begin?

Anyway, I was so upset that I forgot to use hand sanitizer. I had never, ever forgotten to use hand sanitizer before! Oh boy, would I regret that lapse in judgment. On my way home from work that night, Michele sent me a text with a shopping list for things to get at the local "supercenter." I was walking around the store getting the items when I started sweating and my stomach started cramping bad. It was not good! I started walking faster and faster toward the bathroom, and let's just say, I did not make it! Upchuck all over the place! I felt so bad for the employee who had to clean that up. Needless to say, I left without the items, as I was in a hurry. I got home, showered, and went to bed because I was thinking I must have gotten a bug or something. During the night, I went from bad to worse. I started shivering so bad that Michele literally had to put eight blankets on me, and I was still cold.

The next morning, we went to our local walk-in clinic because my primary doctor couldn't get me in, and I was so bad that they sent me to the ER! They said it was because their tests showed that my liver levels were off, and the hospital would be able to do a different test to see what was happening with my liver. I was diagnosed with norovirus and E. coli. Let me repeat that: I was diagnosed with norovirus and E. coli from that house, and my supervisor didn't think we should remove those children! I was so sick that I was admitted and spent three nights in the hospital. The doctor said that norovirus is like what some get on a cruise ship, but I feel like I got screwed because we have never been on a cruise, and I still got it! While I was in the hospital, they did an ultrasound on my liver because my levels were off, and during the ultrasound, they noticed that my gallbladder was full of gallstones. The doctor was amazed that I was able to handle the pain after I ate each meal; I told him that after I had gastric bypass surgery, I didn't eat very much and that I had assumed that the pain was related to that, so I ignored it. I had gotten to the point where I was only eating one meal a day at night, and I still do this today because of the discomfort caused by those gallstones. Well, a surgeon came by and asked, "Hey, you want to get that gallbladder removed?" He meant after I was well, of course, and so a month later on December 1, 2016, I went in for a "simple" outpatient procedure to have my gallbladder removed. I woke up and was told that all had gone well, and don't remember anything else.

Well, I remember what Michele told me anyway. Between December 1 and 5, something went horribly wrong, to say the least. Michele told me that on the third, I started to feel ill much like I did a month prior with the norovirus and the E. coli. By December 5, I was on the toilet not able to move or speak at times. So, Michele and Greyson got me out of the bathroom and laid me in the bed. Michele called the doctor's office and explained that I was just not with it. I was hallucinating and talking about things that didn't make sense. The nurse told her to bring me in at 1:30 p.m. The way that the nurse handled the call made it sound like a routine situation, and Michele felt that maybe she was overreacting. Finally, Michele got to the point that she would rather take me to the hospital and be overreacting than have something bad happen to me. They put me into the van. She recalled that it was incredibly hard because my legs would lock up or freeze at times. So, there I was in the front seat of the van, not communicating, and Michele was speeding to the local emergency room with my dad in the back seat of the van.

This next little part is actually kind of funny. When we got to the emergency room, Michele and my dad jumped out and asked the valet to get a nurse. They returned with a wheelchair, but the van was too far from the curb to get me into it. Michele was trying to pull me out when the nurses told her to stop because I was a big guy and they didn't want her to get hurt or to have me fall. So, they asked her to move the van to the ramp to make it easier. Michele pushed my legs into the van and then closed the door. She asked the valet for the key; unfortunately, the valet she had given the keys to had put them in his pocket and gone to get a car for a patient who was leaving. So, Michele had to wait to move the van. It was warm, and when Michele tried to open the door to the van, she noticed it was locked. She tried telling me to unlock the doors, but I was so out of it, I just stared out the front windshield. She started banging on the window, but nothing helped. The nurses were all waiting with Michele and my dad for the valet. One of the nurses said that this was like the Twilight Zone. And it really was! Finally, the valet came back, and they got the van moved and me out. They took me straight into a trauma room.

They started hooking me up to everything while Michele was explaining to the doctor about my recent surgery and how I had been acting the last couple of days. She had to do all the talking because I was so out of it. Apparently, I was so bad that they put a central venous catheter line in through my groin, and I didn't even flinch. Michele said the scene was like one on the popular television show *ER*. Everyone was scrambling. One doctor made her feel so bad by asking her why she hadn't brought me in sooner. She explained to him that when she called the surgeon's office, the nurse made it seem like it was no big deal—that this was routine. She felt so bad about delaying going to the hospital, and I truly feel that this has played a major part in her current struggle with agoraphobia and anxiety.

So, December 5 will always my "Death Day." Shortly after they made Michele leave the trauma room, I passed away from six system failures caused by severe septic shock. The surgeon who did my "routine" gallbladder removal had sliced a duct, and bile was leaking into my body and causing to me to become very ill. Thankfully, the trauma team was able to revive me and give me a second chance at life.

Oh, but the fun didn't end there. I was in a coma for seven days and then in a medically induced coma for another seven days. The medically induced coma was needed because I was still hallucinating and trying to escape my bed; they had to use restraints to strap me to the bed. When I finally woke up, I was extremely upset and disappointed because I realized that the awesome dream I was having was not real! See, I was dreaming that I was a part of a game show and I had won this amazing trip for my family—a once-in-a-lifetime vacation. Michele and I never had a honeymoon; we have never been out of the country or had any dream vacation. So, when I woke up, I was really sad. The other bad news was I had to learn how to walk again and write my name, and that sucked. And I kept seeing these pesky black spirit things in the corners of my room, which were scaring the crap out of me, so I tried to sleep most of the time.

Michele was with me every day, and I wish I could have rewarded her with sweet and loving words, but apparently, according to her, I was not very nice to her when I came out of my coma. See, Michele is half Korean, and so it seems I kept calling her a North Korean and being mean to her. The strange thing was that the doctors and nurses thought I was hilarious. Don't judge me as Michele and I do poke fun at each other from time to time (all the time), but this time, she was taking it seriously. Michele was fearful that all

I had gone through might have changed me and my personality; she thought maybe the "new" Jon didn't love her. She still reminds me of this, by the way.

I spent almost a month in the hospital. I suffered from memory loss, hallucinations, loss of words, and dizziness for some time. Even after almost two years, I still have short-term memory loss issues, but I learned to manage because the alternative was being six feet underground. Can I complain?

The saddest part was when I came home and saw the kids. They were excited and cheering, and I knew their faces, but I couldn't remember their names. Oh, I felt so bad, so low and depressed. I had Michele take me to bed and tell the kids I had to lie down. Thankfully, their names came back to me quickly because I couldn't play that off forever. The best part of short-term memory loss was watching movies that I had forgotten that I had already watched. We watched all the movies we owned, so I was a cheap date. I'm thankful Michele can watch movies over and over and not complain. Physically, I wasn't getting better as I should have been either, but that was because there was a mix-up with the physical therapy. We thought that the hospital was going to set it up, and they thought my primary doctor was going to set it up, so it never got done. Eventually, that was resolved after Michele took matters into her own hands to make sure it was set up. I went through a few months of in-home therapy and then a couple of months of occupational therapy to get ready to go back to work.

Finally, Back to Work in 2017

So, let's recount how long I was out of work and the toll that had on my family emotionally, spiritually, and financially. I went back to work in August 2017. I had been off work for nine months, and my FMLA had run out in January 2017 because I had been off work in 2016 for the thyroid cancer treatments. If it had not been for family and friends, I don't know what would have happened. Some of our dearest friends put on a fund-raiser and a GoFundMe campaign for us, and it was just love that got us through.

I went back to work, but something in me was different, and honestly, how could I be the same? I mean, how could anyone be the same after dying? The way I looked at life, Michele, my kids, and everything was different. It's not that I didn't value life before, but after my traumatic experiences,

I truly valued life as God values life—as in, all life has value. I stopped to smell the roses, literally. I took pictures of the clouds with the sun's rays breaking through or the kids playing with toys with goofy smiles on their faces. I began to appreciate everything for the first time in my 46 years. Michele noticed this and came to me one day and said, "Hey, if you want to move back to Texas, we can." I was floored, as these were the words that I had been wanting to hear for 20 years! To me, there is no place like Texas.

So, I immediately started looking for work, and because child protective service agencies always need employees, it wasn't a matter of when but where I wanted to work and live. It wasn't long before I was notified of a couple of interviews, and I took Keegan and Ian with me to Texas, leaving Michele home with Kai and the dogs. My parents, brother, and his family live in the same town, so I knew they would be okay while I was gone. The interviews went well, and I had to choose between two office locations—one in Waco and the other in Temple. I definitely chose the right location.

In August 2017, we moved from Florida to Texas; it was an exhausting move, but it was so very worth it to be back home. Not only was it great to be home, but working for the state of Texas was like being on vacation compared to working for CPS in Florida. But the honeymoon was short-lived. At first, everything was great, and we loved the new house and living in Texas, but things with Keegan started unraveling quickly. Keegan, who was 11, began throwing temper tantrums worse than his five-year-old brother, kicking and screaming to the point of growling and grunting when he did not get his way. Any amount of discipline would make it worse and just seemed to send him over the edge. It was doing the same to Michele.

This was just the beginning of our unexpected journey . . .

CHAPTER 2

KEEGAN'S STORY

It might not seem logical to start with Keegan's story since this book is largely about me and my journey, but if it hadn't been for Keegan's journey, none of my life would make sense. Keegan is our miracle child, at least that is what we have always called him. See, there is such a large age gap between him and our two oldest children, Alana and Greyson—almost 10 years in fact. Michele and I didn't think we could have any more children after years of trying; we just figured it wasn't in the cards for us. Since we didn't think we could have any more kids, we stopped using all forms of birth control. I mean, hey, after almost 10 years of trying and nothing, what was the point of wasting money, especially when we didn't have any.

When Keegan was conceived, I had just had gastric bypass surgery. I was still on social security disability and volunteering as a youth pastor at a church plant in our area. When Michele and I found out that we were expecting, it was exciting, especially for me for a lot of reasons. As I said, I had recently had gastric bypass surgery, and I was losing weight and losing it fast. My heaviest known weight was 525 pounds, which was recorded on the morning of my surgery. I was most excited because Keegan was going to be my first child who wouldn't know me as the "fat" dad. The dad who couldn't do anything. The dad who hid away because people would point or stare when I went outside. Once, a child came up to me in a store, pointed at me, and called me a monster. Yeah, you can imagine how awesome that felt and what that did to my self-esteem. So, for a while, I hid away from the world, even my family. I basically lived in my room. I had it all—TV, video games, and DVD player—so, I had no reason to leave. But as I began losing weight, I was regaining my mobility, so I was going to be the "active" dad that I hadn't been for the older children. I felt horrible about that. I mean, seriously, I don't think anyone grows up saying to themselves, "I'm going to have kids and then hide away in my bedroom and balloon up to almost 600 pounds."

With the weight loss and the new baby coming, I was having so many exciting new possibilities and dreams, and Keegan wasn't even here yet. I think that hope comes with the news of expecting the birth of a child. But also, for me, it was like a second chance at being a parent, and I was determined not to waste it. It was also very cool to see how Alana and Greyson were just as excited as we were that we were having another baby. Alana was hoping for a sister, and Greyson of course wanted a little brother that he could teach how to play baseball. Everyone seemed to have their own dreams laid out for Keegan, and he wasn't even here yet.

We have a roughly 10-year gap between the "groups" of kids. First, we had Alana and Greyson, and then, we had Keegan, Ian, and Kai. Once we found out that Michele was pregnant, we started collecting baby stuff because we had gotten rid of everything that we had from Alana and Greyson. The pregnancy was not the easiest for Michele. She ended up with gestational diabetes, and I felt so bad for her. She had to stay on a strict diet, and if the craving did not fit in the diet plan, she was not able to have it. Personally, I cannot imagine having only one piece of pizza for dinner, but that is all she would get if we had pizza. Needless to say, we did not have pizza very often, and as a youth pastor, it was an oddity to not have pizza frequently.

Finally, the doctors induced her a week early because of the gestational diabetes, and Keegan had to spend the first few days in the NICU. His body had difficulty regulating his temperature, and the medical staff wanted to monitor his blood sugar to make sure he did not have any issues due to the gestational diabetes. Michele did her best to breastfeed. She would go to the NICU every three hours to feed him, but the nurses told her he was not getting enough milk, so they started to supplement. It was so heartbreaking for Michele because she had always had difficulty with breastfeeding. After

Keegan came home, she continued to nurse him and supplement. Eventually, he developed a rash; it looked like burns on his skin. The rash was so bad; I had never seen anything like it. He always had to wear socks on his hands, and he would constantly rub his little face. The doctor told us that the problems was an allergic reaction to milk. They said he would likely grow out of it by the time he was one year old. Until then, he had to drink a special formula that was partially digested; Michele also had to cut milk from her diet, and boy was she miserable. I could not believe how many things have milk in them. It's crazy! Thank goodness Keegan eventually grew out of his milk allergy. Unfortunately, he remained a very picky eater until this last year for some strange reason, but hey, we aren't complaining.

Keegan was always so smart, and he got away with everything. The kids in the youth group that I led loved him and would let him do anything he wanted. He was most definitely a spoiled baby. He had a lot of problems with ear infections, and the antibiotics the doctors used to treat him caused yeast infections. Poor baby's bottom was always hurting. Finally, we were able to get the ear infections under control, but it took months. When we moved out of our house, they found a leak under the tub, and mold was everywhere. Poor Keegan was reacting to the mold, but once we moved, we did not have any more issues with those problems.

By the time Keegan turned four, we noticed that his speech was not where it should be. We had him evaluated, and he had to go through speech therapy. He really loved speech therapy; they would play games, and his speech improved. Although his speech was not on par with other kids his age, he showed a noticeable improvement. His therapist didn't think she could do any more for him, so they graduated him from the program. During this time, we learned that Keegan was having issues with allergies.

This time, his allergies weren't just food-related; they were caused by seasonal elements, which led to a host of problems. He had constant fluid behind the eardrum, and that caused his hearing to be distorted. Doctors started Keegan on three types of allergy medication and then a second round of speech therapy. The allergist told us that Keegan was allergic to many things, but the biggest issue was that he was allergic to things in every season, so he never got any relief. Keegan's allergist worked on his condition for about a year and not only did his allergies get better, but his speech improved tremendously. Finally, Keegan seemed like every other child except for one thing. He always looked ill; Michele and I worried that he was going to be "sickly" because he had pasty white skin, and his eyes had what looked to be dark rings around them. Keegan actually looked like a certain Lord of the Rings character, Gollum. Yes, yes, I know that is horrible; we were not the ones who first made that comparison, but sadly, it stuck. In our defense, he was a very cute and lovable Gollum. Keegan was a riot; he was so funny and kept us entertained.

As Keegan grew, he was very thin and taller than most of the kids his age. In preschool, he was so loved by his teachers; he was their little sweetheart, and he always wanted to help them with whatever they were doing. Keegan was a busybody and had a hard time sitting in one place and staying on task, but everyone would say, "He's just being a boy" or "He's just at that age." We completely agreed with that and still do agree to a certain extent, but knowing what we know now, we wish we had made different choices or that we had actually made some choices. Sometimes, making no choice is worse than acting and being wrong, as in our case with Keegan.

As time went on, we noticed that Keegan had a few quirks, and once school started, things got worse. Michele was getting calls from school saying that Keegan was either causing trouble or getting hurt. You know there is a problem when you have the school phone number memorized. Keegan's school was one of those where students have to wait to get in because there are so few openings. The school was relatively small, and that was part of its charm and desirability. The older students had classes in the same building as the younger students. We never thought that was going to be a part of the issue until we started having problems with Keegan—especially with how strict they were. Keegan rode the bus, and it was their policy for the bus driver and the bus attendant to segregate the children according to their age. Sadly, there was some confusion on Keegan's bus. Keegan, who should have been at the front of the bus was allowed to ride in the rear of the bus with eighth graders, but Keegan was just starting second grade. Well, on this bus, the kids were stealing his books or "borrowing" them as they were his "friends," and Keegan ultimately got suspended off the bus because some of the older children got him to ask a young girl if she would have sex with him. Keegan didn't know what sex was or what he was asking her. We hadn't had that talk with him yet.

After that suspension was over, the final nail in the coffin came when they lost Keegan. Yes, they lost Keegan! One day, Keegan didn't get off the bus at his usual stop. I asked the little girl who always got off with him at the bus stop if she had seen him. She said that she had not, so of course, we started freaking out. There are rare times in life when you feel this dread that happens in your stomach, and this was one of those times. We called the school, and no one could find him, and then we called the transportation department to try to find him. The school and the transportation department were on high alert for the possibility that Keegan was lost. As the bus driver was pulling into the bus barn where they lock up the busses overnight, the driver slammed on the brakes, and that knocked the sleeping Keegan off his seat and onto the floor. If not for the driver slamming on the brakes, Keegan would have been locked on a bus all night.

So, after months of dealing with the school to no avail, we decided to pull him out and homeschool him. Okay, I hear some of you saying, "Well, that's not enough to pull a kid out of school." Let me run down some of the issues that we had with him since day one of kindergarten: crawling under bathroom stalls (numerous times), looking under bathroom stalls, touching, talking, and a host of other things that he did not have permission to do. Sadly, some of his actions could have gotten him in big trouble, but thankfully the school personnel truly liked him and went easy on him. Maybe they knew something about Keegan before we did and were just more patient with him.

Michele was able to switch to a three-day work schedule to homeschool our children. That meant that she had to work 40 hours in three days, but you have to do what you have to do for the ones you love. With Keegan at home full time, we started noticing that Keegan was not like other children. First, we noticed that Ian was gaining ground on his brother academically and was more mature as well. We know that maturity can vary from one child to another, but we were seeing a huge difference between the two brothers. Since we were homeschooling, we figured that we could deal with the gap and cope with it ourselves.

Then, I started noticing changes in Michele. She was crying out of frustration and was not as patient as she normally was with the kids. Being the fixer, I tried to fix the problem myself, and that just made things worse with Michele and with Keegan's situation. I didn't listen to Michele, and that made Keegan's problem worse because it compounded it. Ultimately, we had to admit that we needed help, and we had to admit that our son needed help. That may have been the hardest part. It was humbling, to say the least.

With the insurance that we had at the time, everything had to go through his primary care doctor, and we were blessed to have an incredible team of physicians who loved us for many years. So, we reached out to them and received some sage advice along with a referral to a neuropsychologist for testing. The testing took numerous hours, but we were glad that we got it done; then, we had to wait for the results. We would have gotten the results back quicker but getting the follow-up appointment was the issue. If you have tried to get a child in to see a psychologist or psychiatrist, you know that the wait can be up to seven or nine months depending on your area. Unfortunately, the need for these services has skyrocketed over the past few years. Keegan's test results revealed ADHD, anxiety disorder, ODD (oppositional defiant disorder), and some depression. Keegan started counseling with the psychologist who did the testing; he was local, but we had to drive 75 miles for Keegan to see the psychiatrist. The psychiatrist said it was better to work on the anxiety issue first since the medications used to treat ADHD would work against the medications for the other problems.

With the kids being homeschooled, we adjusted our schedule to help work with Keegan's ADHD, and thankfully the medicine seemed to help his emotional state. By August 2017, we were going through many changes as we prepared to move to Texas. Thankfully, the doctor was able give Keegan some refills hoping that it would be enough until we could get established with another doctor after we moved. This is when we learned about the seven- to nine-month waiting lists for psychologists and psychiatrists. Sadly, there is such a high demand for child psychologists and psychiatrists in Texas, and everywhere for that matter. One good thing, well actually two: first, our new insurance went into effect sooner than expected, and second, Keegan's new primary care doctor was very understanding and worked with us until Keegan could be seen by specialists at McLane Children's Clinic in Temple, TX.

Nevertheless, there were some problems, actually a lot of them. Despite being so excited about being in Texas and loving our new home and everything about Texas, Keegan started having meltdowns. Not temper tantrums—I'm talking full-blown meltdowns that lasted anywhere from an hour to half a day! These meltdowns could be over anything—from something small to something major, but the result was the same. There was no difference between something minor or major; if you walked in on one of his meltdowns, you would think someone was killing him or that someone had just died. That was how bad they were. They were scary. Keegan would scream, cry, moan, yell, and make animal noises almost like he was possessed. He would call Michele names, yell at us, scream at us, and everything in between. He scared everyone in the house. To this day, when Keegan has a meltdown, Ian will ask, "Is Keegan going to be okay?" How sad is that? A brother should not have to be asking that; it just breaks our hearts.

Keegan's meltdowns intensified and continued for several months. The meltdowns also had an odd pattern. First, he would start by crying; then, the outburst would intensify to screaming for a while, then moaning and groaning. After he got it all out of his system, he would come back out and apologize. You are probably thinking, "That's great; he is remorseful." Yes, that is great, but this is also where it gets odd. He would apologize, but it would be so over-the-top and almost comical. In response, I would tell him, "It is okay. I love you. It is going to be okay" because he would start saying that maybe we would be better off without him. Then, Keegan would go into his grand finale! He always ended with his "disclosure moment," by telling on himself. His psychologist thinks he does this because he loves and craves the drama. He seemed to feel let down when we did not punish him after he told on himself. I think the most we have ever done was not let him use any internet device when he disclosed that he was looking at pornography.

This pattern continued for a while. One day while I was at work, I started getting text messages, which was not abnormal, but I could not answer them because I was conducting an interview at work. But the messages kept coming, and the last text from Michele said, "I need you to call me NOW!" Needless to say, I excused myself from doing the interview and called her only to hear her crying and telling me that Keegan was suicidal. That felt like an unbelievable kick in the stomach. I know that young kids think about suicide, and some even commit suicide. Working with CPS, I deal with these situations all the time, but this was my kid. This was my Keegan! Thankfully, my coworker was able to take over with the interviews, and I rushed home to be with Keegan. I remember driving home and just crying to God, "Why? Haven't we gone through enough?" Oh, I was so mad at God that I was screaming at Him, but I knew it wasn't Him; He wasn't to blame. I could feel His presence tell me, "Jon, it is going to be okay. I can take it. I am with you." So, by the time I got home, I was at peace, and I was able to talk with Keegan, but he was at the point where some intervention was needed. Keegan was begging for me to take him to a hospital to get help because he recognized that he needed medical help. It was heartbreaking to sit with him and hold him and to hear my 10-year-old son tell me that he wanted to end his life, that he did not have any hope, and that it was all lost. Then, I looked around and saw Ian crying because he was so worried about his big brother. Ian is such a big-hearted kid. Michele and my parents were crying because they felt helpless. We all saw this hurting child, but we could not fix the problem; it made me feel absolutely worthless and small at that moment.

Keegan, Michele, and I got into my car and headed off to get him the only help we knew of at that moment. We went to Sonic and got him his favorite food and had some good laughs before taking him to the hospital for intake. I knew what was coming. I have done this for kids in CPS, and it is not an easy thing. When we got to the hospital, the mood changed from laughter to gloom. Keegan was holding his mom's hand, and I had my arm around him walking up to the hospital. I asked him, "Keegan, are you sure you need to be here?" He looked me in the eye and said, "Yes, sir." We walked up to the desk and told them why we were there, and then we were told to sit in the lobby for what seemed like an eternity before being called back.

This is when the mood went from somber to nightmare! First, they did the medical part of the examination just as if we were at the ER for any other reason. Then, they did the preliminary psychological exam to determine whether to admit Keegan, offer an outpatient option, or take no action. Well,

Michele and I were there to hear the answers as the intake person asked Keegan questions to understand his status, and the situation went from bad to worse. Michele and I were weeping. Not crying. Weeping. What did we hear? Not only was Keegan suicidal, but he had been hearing voices and seeing things for some time and had not told us. We were hearing this in front of strangers for the first time. Oh, it gets worse. Then, she asked, "Have you ever attempted suicide?" We were thinking—or at least I was thinking—the answer would be no; then, I was shocked to hear that answer was yes and that he had tried to hang himself two years before. They asked us if we knew this, and I think I almost cussed and said, "F- no," but I did not. We just said, "Of course not." If you have never been where we have been, try to imagine that your 10-year-old just said that when he was eight, he had tried to hang himself. What? Really? I was beside myself with sadness and confusion because Keegan was always so happy and goofy. When you hear something like that, you automatically try to remember, "Okay, what was happening two years ago that would have made him so unhappy that he would have wanted to hang himself?"

Needless to say, after these revelations, he was admitted to the hospital. Saying good-bye was so hard, but man, it gets harder. Michele and I left the hospital, and I don't think we said one word on the way home. I called my boss and told her what happened and told her that I was taking some time off; she completely understood and said that she was praying for Keegan and us. The next day, we went back to the hospital to meet with the psychiatrists who would be working with Keegan, to go over background information and so on. We were told that we wouldn't be able to see him at that time as visitation was later that night. We had a good meeting, and as we were leaving, we heard this familiar yell, "Mom, Dad!" Then, we heard a woman's voice say, "Get back into line!" When we turned around, we saw Keegan, and we both started crying. Then, he asked if he could hug us because they were required to walk in straight lines with their hands behind their backs. After he got permission, he ran to us and gave us a big hug. It was the best hug ever. It was so hard to let go, but we knew we had to. Every night, we went to the hospital to see him, and we would play card games. After he was there a while, he would sit at the table and cry for us to let him come home. It was truly grueling to go through this with him every night when it was time to go. During the day, we went to the hospital and met with the treating doctors and staff to discuss his diagnoses and their struggles with him.

Keegan spent over a week in the hospital and was diagnosed with ASD (autism spectrum disorder), ADHD, anxiety, depression, and borderline personality disorder with auditory and visual hallucinations. When you hear doctors say such things about your child, it is jarring to say the least, especially when you did not know he was struggling with some of these issues. Sadly, we also learned how badly he had been mistreated. The school that we had waited so long to get him into was part of the problem. Keegan was bullied on a daily basis: basketballs thrown at him and landing near his head, kids stealing from him, and name-calling. Why did we never hear about this? Because these things were done by Keegan's "friends." Keegan thinks everyone is his friend, so if you talk with him one time, you are his best friend. This leaves Keegan wide open for being mistreated by kids or adults who do not have the best intentions. This is why we have to be so careful with him when he is playing video games on the internet because we have found messages on the Xbox in which he had told people where we live and so on. It is so scary that he doesn't understand that not everyone is his friend. He gets taken advantage of all the time on the new Fortnite game by being suckered into trades in which he gives up all his stuff first, and then the other person doesn't give him anything in return. Next thing you know, he slams the controller down and cries to us, saying, "But he is my friend; why would he do that to me?" We explain to him that not everyone is his friend, and of course, he says he understands, but we know it will happen again.

One of the other big issues with Keegan is that he wants to go back to public school. He wants friends so badly. We are so torn; but he is not ready to be back in that setting. What has made it worse is that Keegan has regressed in his behavior. Even Kai, his five-year-old brother, doesn't throw fits like Keegan does, and as a former teacher, I know that most teachers will not put up with this distraction. I refuse to have him in a special education class because some of the students in those classes would influence him in a very bad way. Special education classes include kids whose challenges range from being nonverbal to exhibiting behavioral issues. For some reason, Keegan would flock to the kids who have behavioral problems, or they would pick on him because they would see him as an easy target. The doctors stated that even though Keegan can carry on an adult conversation and knows about adult things, he is still very innocent. They all said that he has this innocence about him that affects how he sees the world and people. For Keegan, everyone is good, and he has no sense of danger. He has always been that way; we just thought he was going to be an adrenaline junkie. Keegan also has no filter! Oh my gosh, he says what's on his mind, even to adults. It has caused many problems and even ruined relationships with some people, but we will always choose our son over others.

Keegan sees a psychologist weekly, and he sees his psychiatrist monthly for his medicine checks and to see whether there have been any major events since the last visit. His psychologist works with him on his daily routine and tries to help him find ways to cope so that, maybe, one day, he can go back to school. The psychologist and psychiatrist agree that sending Keegan back to school now would be detrimental to him, and we agree with this assessment. We are blessed that his team truly cares about Keegan; that means a lot to us. They recently sent him to classes that would help him improve his social skills with other kids his age, and that was a disaster. The kids were like the ones in the special education classes that we didn't want him hanging around. The kids made fun of him and called him names because he answered all the questions that the teacher would ask. See, Keegan is a people pleaser; he loves to make people happy. So, he has always been the teacher's pet, so to speak, as far back as preschool. Well, some of the kids didn't like that he was answering all the questions, and he would come out all dejected to the point of crying. Needless to say, he refused to go after three times. As a parent, what can you say to your child when this type of thing keeps happening? He doesn't understand why people do such things to him. He just cries to us that he doesn't understand why he is different and why he does what he does. Keegan is truly at war with himself and little does he know that I know exactly how he feels.

Nowadays, Keegan sleeps in our room most nights because he is scared of his room or of being alone anywhere. It also makes me feel more comfortable that he is in our room because he still has dark moments that we have to talk him through. He just recently went to a sleep doctor because since he has been sleeping with us, we noticed that he isn't sleeping well. We think that he might have sleep apnea. Keegan has had night terrors since he was quite young. If your child has never had a night terror, you should thank the Lord right now because they are not a fun experience. He mainly gets them now when he is sick for some reason, so when he gets sick, we prepare ourselves for the worst and pray for the best. This past weekend, Keegan had one of his worst weekends to date. He was seeing and hearing things that were not just coming for him but for us as well. It was truly a horrifying weekend. That following Monday, we met with his psychiatrist and one of his colleagues to go over what had happened, and we played a recording of Keegan in the midst of an episode. Michele and I both were scared that they were going to admit Keegan right there by the way they were talking. But they decided it was best to put him back on a medication that they had recently taken him off because of unhealthy weight gain. Then, the very next day, Keegan had an appointment with his psychologist who discussed some issues with us that we had been privately concerned about. We talked about Keegan's future—about whether he will be able to be on his own when he is an adult. We also talked about getting respite care, especially for Michele. So, as you read this, please pray for Keegan, as he is still on his journey.

Keegan asked, "Why did God make me this way? I don't want to be this way."

But it was because of Keegan's story that my eyes were opened, and I found answers to so many questions that I have been asking as long as I can remember. Keegan's story also answers some questions about our other son Greyson, my father, and possibly my older brother.

Next, the birth of a legend . . . just kidding.

CHAPTER 3

HOW MY JOURNEY BEGAN

I was born in April 1971. Nixon was president, Disney World opened, and Russia and the United States made several key space launches. Hey, it was a great year, what can I say? Most of all, I made my presence known or felt depending on whom you ask. I was the youngest of three children born to Don and Judy Locke. I have an older brother, Don Jr., who everyone lovingly called Donnie Jr. most of his life, which I'm sure he loved. My older sister, Mary, was called Mary Margaret, which I'm also sure she loved—I hope you all can read the sarcasm in that. I loved being called by my first and middle name because it sounded cool, almost French, "Jon Paul." But I was only called that when I was in trouble, which means I heard it often. We lived in the most perfect little subdivision in Northeast Houston called Royalwood. Well, at least I thought it was perfect. To me, it was perfect because all my friends were there, and I knew everyone. Plus, I grew up in a time when parents would say, "Just be home by the time the streetlights come on." Man, we would ride our bikes and play in the woods for hours upon hours. The weird thing about childhood is how our perceptions of things change as we get older. For instance, I thought our home in Royalwood was huge, but it was less than 1500 square feet, and you think that the Alamo is huge until you go back as an adult and realize that it's tiny. If you have been there as a child and then go again as an adult, you know exactly what I mean.

I hear some people speak of their childhood and their picture-perfect memories; I do not remember much of my childhood. I have some kind of block, and it frustrates me so much. Therapists and psychologists say there could be a number of reasons for my memory gap, including some kind of traumatic event. Sadly, I just don't know. What I do know is that a lot of my childhood memories come from pictures and what people have told me. I grew up in a loving Christian home and always knew I was loved by my mom. I am not sure if my dad knew how to show love. Dad's way of showing love was by providing things; he was not always there. He was a truck driver who delivered new cars mainly for General Motors, so I always got to see and sit in the new cars before anyone else, and I loved it. I love, love, love cars! I mean, cars were and are my thing. This may sound weird, but I loved the smell of my dad when he would get home; yeah, he was dirty and smelly, but he was home. As a child, I guess that all I wanted was love and admiration from my father. I think in some ways I still chase this, even though I think I have it.

What is my earliest memory—not one that someone told me about or something I saw in a picture but an actual memory? It's probably a toss-up among three events. First, I remember being at a ceremony at Royalwood Elementary for my brother's Boy Scout troop, and my mother was telling me that this would be my school the next year. I remember being very excited about that. Second, when I was a little older, I was walking to school with friends when I took a dare that almost ended in disaster. Behind our house was a path that we took to school; the path was cut through the grass and had a canal running beside it. Well, some of my friends dared me to walk next to the water or something to that effect. The banks of the canal were steep and packed dirt, so it was tricky to walk on. I started fine, but then I started to slide down—slowly at first, and then I started to panic, which made me slide faster. I thought, "Man, I can't get wet, 'cause then my mom will know, and I'll be in trouble." My sister was coming through the gate by our house with some of her friends, so I thought, "Oh crap, she will tell on me!" Then, my friend Mike screamed, "Snakes!" Two large coral snakes were swimming my way. My sister saw me, and she freaked out and ran over to me; then our mutual friend Danny went and got my mom. They eventually linked arms and pulled me up by my lunch box. It truly scared the pee out of me. Yep, I had to go change my clothes!

How My Journey Began

The third memory was when I broke my arm. We were playing football in the front yard, and I went to get the ball, and as I was getting up, my sister jumped on my back. Here is either the funny thing or the horrible thing. My mom was having a Tupperware party at our house that night, so they either didn't have time to tend to me or didn't believe that my arm was seriously hurt. During the party, my dad and us kids had to stay in the bedroom. I was still crying because I was in a lot of pain, so my dad decided to test me. He knew that I loved money. So, he had me put my good arm behind my back and then he hung a dollar in front of me and said, "Grab it." When I couldn't grab it, he knew something was wrong with my arm. Needless to say, they took me to the ER—after the Tupperware party, of course. The arm was broken, so I got a cast and a bunch of toys because I milked that one for a long time!

Maybe you are seeing some similarities between my childhood behavior and Keegan's. Unfortunately, this is just the beginning. I was the teacher's pet in school (this embarrassment continued for my mom for many years), but I was already doing things that others dared me to do, exhibiting risky behaviors, and just wanting to be loved.

My happy childhood took a turn for the worse when I was around eight years of age. We moved across Highway 90 and, although it was only a two-mile move, it put us in a different school zone, which meant that I moved to a different school in the middle of the school year. I left all my friends and everything I was comfortable with. We moved from a house in a subdivision to a one-acre lot with a brand-new double-wide trailer. Don't get me wrong; it was awesome. The whole back of our property was wooded, and it was so much fun to play on. It was not fun to mow with a push mower, but my parents tried to make that fun for us by doing races around the property to make mowing it bearable. We also knew our neighbors, as my parents were founding members of a church plant, so that was good. Well, partially good, anyway; I will explain more later.

This was the year I got hepatitis A. Oh, what a joy that was. I just remember being at Dairy Queen as usual after church one Sunday night where a lot of the church families went after Sunday night service. I was sitting across from my mom, and she noticed that the whites of my eyes were yellow. So, she asked some of the other parents what they thought was wrong, and they didn't know what it was, but they told her that she should take me to a doctor the next day. I don't remember how long I was laid up, but I do remember eating a lot of hard candy for some reason, and I gained a lot of weight. Finally, it was determined that I must have gotten hepatitis A from a water fountain at church because a lady from our church had it.

Moving in the middle of the school year was hard for me. The good thing was I knew a lot of the kids in my new class from church and from little league sports. Because of my grades at my other school, I was placed in the "smart kids" class, but there was a problem with that. They were more advanced, and I had missed quite a bit of school while I was sick, so I was coming in blind so to speak. There I was socially awkward, nervous, and feeling stupid, so what was I to do? Put on my clown costume and start entertaining the class, and that is what I did. Boy, did I do that well! I did it so well that at the year-end awards ceremony I won class clown. Yeah, baby! Yes, my mom was there to witness this. Honestly, it was all I had, folks!

I was told that I was a smart kid blah–blah–blah; "Jon just doesn't apply himself." Yeah, I've heard that a million times. My mom heard this at every parent-teacher conference and every time I got in trouble at school, which was often back in the day when they took a piece of wood to your behind. Some of my teachers had us sign our names, or they would drill holes in their paddles for greater aerodynamics. The coaches used to make us get down in football stances for optimum leverage on the buttocks. Unlike a lot of people in prison, I admit I did it and deserved every single swat!

One thing that some people said I was good at was singing. I loved music and I loved singing; music was one of the few classes that I looked forward to. I felt like I belonged in there, like I fit in; I was wanted. That was the only class in which I didn't get in trouble. The other cool thing about the class was that my teacher was friends with the drummer of the legendary band ZZ Top, and I actually got to meet them, so that was cool. But there was a downside to this class, and it was a very big downside. I learned about racism, serious racism. We were preparing for the year-end talent show, and the teacher wanted some acts to sign up. Journey's "Open Arms" was the big hit, so my friend and I wanted to sing it as a duet. We went to the teacher at the end of class to sign up, and she said that we couldn't sing that song and that we would have to sing something else. She didn't give any reason but just said that we could not sing it. I went home upset and talked to my mom about it, so she called the teacher. Come to find out that the teacher did not think that some in the audience could handle the fact that a white child and a black child would be singing a love song. It was heartbreaking, and it is still heartbreaking to me. From that day on, I never sang for her again; I lost all respect for her because I did not know anyone who was a racist, so maybe she was the one who could not handle the fact that two kids were singing a song. It was just a song, and it was the 1980s not the 1950s for goodness' sake. Yes, I am still bitter over this because I think part of what I truly loved died that day. I mean that is some heavy stuff for an eight- or nine-year-old to hear or try to understand.

I continued to struggle through elementary school; once or twice, my parents actually begged the school to pass me. They should have let them keep me back; that would have been very beneficial, but I understand why they did it. They did not want me to be embarrassed I'm sure, or even possibly, having me passed to the next grade saved them from some embarrassment, who knows. I think if one of my kids failed a grade, I would be embarrassed if I were being honest. If we are being honest with each other, would you be embarrassed if your kid failed a grade? No judgment here.

I can remember suffering in some of my classes, especially in one math class. I think it was fourth grade math. It was absolutely dreadful for me. Every day, this teacher picked me out to screw with me because early on in the year, I got in huge trouble and he retaliated, which got my parents involved. I do not know what my dad said or did, but the teacher had it in for me the rest of the year. This was one of the classes that I failed, but somehow, I magically passed at the end of the year when report cards came out. I think it was because he did not want to see me again, so he passed me. There was a bright spot in that school year, though. I met the girl—oh man, the girl of my young dreams! We will just call her Mandy. Mandy was the prettiest girl I had seen in my life; she went to my school, and she and her family went to our church. The genetics in this family were insane: She also had beautiful older sisters. I loved her from afar, though, because when it came to the girls,

I was very shy and awkward. But, one day, I found this very nice ring. I think it had a ruby stone in it. So, one Sunday at church, I decided I was going to make my move. I wrote a note, professed my love, and dropped the ring into an envelope. Then, I put said envelope under the windshield wiper of their Suburban. Then, the following Sunday, my mom told me that she had spoken to Mandy's mom who had said, "I guess our kids are getting engaged." Well, that was it; nothing was ever said. Mandy and I never talked about it. She was way out of my league—like, I am on Earth, and she is, like, on the moon; that is how far out of my league she was. Mandy and her family moved to the Kingwood area right after elementary school, and I never saw her again.

Junior high. Oh my gosh, I wish I had fun stories to tell, but there is a reason why this book was originally going to be titled *They Call Me Job.* This is the time in my life when I really started realizing that I was different from everyone else. The best way to describe it is like being uncomfortable in your own skin and not understanding why you feel the way you do. This confusion was a huge struggle, and it was debilitating. It caused my parents to take me to counseling. I don't remember what the specific reasons were, but maybe it had something to do with why they called me "Mad Max." My struggle manifested in extreme depression and intense anger, which caused me to lash out at everyone. Sometimes, I would chase my brother around with tennis racquets or baseball bats, and I would be swinging for the fences! This behavior caused my family to nickname me Mad Max after the character played by Mel Gibson in the movie *Mad Max.* I was a mess, and I was still gaining weight because I found comfort in food. I had a lot of friends—well, I take that back. A lot of people liked me because I was the class clown and the goofball, but I did have a couple of friends. Still no girlfriend and no prospects; well, I had prospects, but they didn't see me as a prospect, LOL.

Man, adolescence was a tough age: I had this puberty thing happening; emotions were running wild; and then on top of that, I felt like I didn't even belong in my own body. Oh boy, did the dark times start happening back then for me. But, honestly, I was too scared to do anything about it, too much of a coward to end it all. That's the way I saw it anyway. There was no thought that my family would be upset or anything like that; I just thought that I had to stop the misery that I was in. I was already conditioned not to go to my parents, or at least not my dad, and well, not my mom either, because the situation would end up with my dad anyway due to the seriousness of it all.

My dad never cried or showed emotion; he was usually this hard exterior of a guy. For example, when I was in fourth grade, I was playing football at a neighbor's house, and a punk kid was there, and I came home crying. I was big for my age and because this kid was my size, my dad made me go back and fight him. I got my butt kicked like there was no tomorrow! He was a ninth grader, so yeah, he had way more experience at fighting than I did. My stomach and back were all black and blue. I got redemption because the neighbor mom brought me home and chewed out my dad, and that equaled a toy shopping spree. Did you catch it earlier when I mentioned that my dad equated being a good parent with being a provider? When he screwed up, he bought me things. Not what I needed in the big picture.

As I was saying, hormones and emotions were running wild, but my problem with school had not changed. Instead of having only one favorite class, I had two: choir and science. Choir would soon change, but science was a favorite because of Ms. P. Wowzers, she was the prettiest teacher I had ever seen; thinking back, she was probably right out of college and nothing like the teachers I had in elementary school. Ms. P made it worth coming to school every day! The problem was I had a lot of competition—as if any of us ever had a chance. You have to remember, a junior high boy's brain does not think rationally, and there were guys who actually fought over her. Boy, were we stupid! Now that I think about it, I didn't have another attractive teacher till high school. Sorry, I was having a flashback to my childhood. The other cool thing about junior high was that our area only had one, so all my old friends had to come to the same school. It was a reunion. But for a lot of my old friends, too much time and distance had passed—that two-mile walk was a killer—so we had drifted apart. The worst thing that happened was that the choir teacher quit, and guess who got the job? Yep, the choir teacher from my elementary school. Ugh, but I needed the credit, so I made the most of it.

I played junior high football for our school, so that was fun; I got a lot of swats from the coaches because I was always goofing around. Getting swats in your practice pants with only a jock strap on is no fun. The coaches in junior high were quite sadistic; they got kicks out of seeing how high they could get us to jump off the ground, I think. It was a different time back in the '80s, though. Coaches could yell and cuss at you, grab you by the face mask and jerk you around, and embarrass the crap out of you. Nowadays, I'm not sure what coaches can say or do without being sued. In Texas, football is king. It doesn't matter whether it's little league or professional football; Texans love their football. My mom has pictures of me sleeping with my football jersey the night before games, which was my ritual. I loved me some football, still do. In junior high, our games were on Thursdays, so we would get to wear our jerseys at school all day, and then, at the end of the day, we would have the big pep rally. Oh, how I loved the pep rallies. The band would be playing, and the cheerleaders would be holding up the huge paper banner, and we would come running through it into the gymnasium. That is, if I was eligible to play. Coaches would get so mad at me because I was the star lineman, so I was needed, wanted. Maybe that is why I loved football so much. But I never got a date to homecoming, never got that first kiss, or held a girl's hand. Everyone liked me, because everyone loves the clown.

In junior high, I also found out that I was very good at tennis. Shocker, right? I mean, for a bigger kid, this was quite the shock to a lot of folks. I was so good, in fact, that I was one of four junior high kids who played on the high school varsity team. I was on the doubles team, but hey, I was still playing up, and that was really cool.

My eighth grade year was a mixed bag of pure crap. No way to sugarcoat it; it was just crap. I was a follower, and I would follow anyone if it meant the possibility of getting a friend. I started doing drugs and drinking my eighth grade year, all with my neighbor. Man, I hated him; he was my nemesis. He was the rich kid who had everything I wanted, and he had the looks and all the girls. We had been friends since we were about five years old; our parents had started the church together. He was at all my birthday parties, and I went to his, and then we ended up moving across the street from him. We were competitive too, even in our lying! He would say something; then, I would have to outdo him, and then he would outdo me. At six years old, he even walked the isle at church to be saved before me, so the next week I did too. He beat me at everything! Man, I hated him! He introduced me to weed; I still remember it like it was yesterday. He brought it over in a prescription bottle, which had three or four "penner" joints in it. We knew how to smoke because we had been practicing when we were younger by smoking grapevines. That was weird because our parents let us, and they would just laugh at us. Boy, have the times changed. Don't remember the high, but I just remember that was my connection. I think he was getting them from his sister's boyfriends, and that's a plural for a reason. Man, it is weird that in pastors' and deacons' families, the kids are just the worst, LOL—okay, not all the kids, but some were, LOL.

Two very tragic things happened: One wasn't tragic, but it followed me to high school, and the other has haunted me my whole life. Both of these events have a lot to do with following the crowd and falling to peer pressure. I just wanted to be accepted and have friends, and what I did was bring my mother unmeasurable amounts of embarrassment, and then I did the same for another mom. First, I will explain the incident with my mom because it doesn't bring up as many horrible feelings as the other incident does. In choir class, we had a substitute for the week, and so everyone was acting crazy. We were all divided into our little groups or cliques. We were in junior high and playing truth or dare. It was my turn, and I picked dare. So, my best friend from my old neighborhood said for me to show a girl my private part. I didn't want to do it, so they started egging me on, including the girl! So, I stuck my right hand down my pants and then unzipped my zipper with my left and stuck out my thumb. Yes! I know the whole thing was stupid and childish, but in my defense, I was stupid and childish. Well, it was done, and everyone had a good laugh, and I don't know if anyone believed it was real, but it didn't matter because I didn't punk out. So, the class ended, and I didn't get in trouble. Then, the last bell rang and still no trouble, so I thought, maybe, "I will be home free." Well, the following Monday, I got called into the office during first period. The girl, who had egged me on to do it told her parents what I did. I was in the principal's office and, of course, no one believed me when I said it was my thumb, and maybe, if I was in the principal's position, I wouldn't have believed me either. Especially, since I had been in and out of his office for three years. What happened next really shook me to my core; they had my mom come get me. I had to explain this to my mother! "Great!" I thought, "Now, my mom thinks I am a pervert, and I didn't even really do it." It was embarrassing for my mom and for me. I think I was grounded for a very long time. But the school punishment was severe too; I was sent to the SAC room. I don't remember what SAC stood for, but it sucked. We would sit in cubicles, in isolation, and no talking for the whole school day. You even had to eat lunch in the cubicle. To add more embarrassment, the teacher who oversaw the SAC room was a deacon at our church, so he knew why I was in there. So yeah, it was just awesome. This happened near the end of the school year; I spent over a month in SAC.

Now to my biggest and most regrettable mistake of my life. There was a kid who had the same first name as me but spelled differently. He was a nice kid, very tall, and an outcast of sorts. Some of my friends were picking on him; they were relentless with the bullying. This young kid was from my old neighborhood, and we had been friends and played on the same little league teams before my family moved. I realize now, of course, that peer pressure is no excuse for my behavior. I have spent my life trying to find him and teaching my children and the youth that God has entrusted me to lead not to be bullies. What I am about to describe makes me sick, and I am feeling an anxiety attack because I know what I am about to write and the judgment that is about to be heaped my way and deservedly so.

My old subdivision had only a few bus stops located at the entrances of the subdivision. So, if you lived in the middle or the back of the subdivision, you had quite a walk ahead of you every day. This particular day was a Friday, and I was going to spend the night with some of my old friends at their home. The bullying started before we even left the school, and John just sat on the bus taking it, and for some reason that makes things worse when someone doesn't fight back. I wasn't doing anything, and then one of my friends said that he made a comment about me or my mom; mom jokes were huge then, and they started razzing me about how I couldn't let him get away with that. So, I started in with the comments; then I started pushing him and pushing him in the back of the head. He never fought back, not once; I think he must have been used to it, which makes this all the worse. The guys started telling him that he was going to get it once we got off the bus and the bus was out of sight, and I could see him getting antsy. We got to the bus stop, which was at the old store called the "U-Totem." The bus stopped, and we got out, and then he got out and started sprinting as fast as he could! We chased him down behind some houses, and everyone circled him so he could not escape. He had to fight me or— I don't know what. I was just hoping that he wouldn't, so we would just go to my friend's house, but they kept egging this on, and it became animalistic. I had only been in one fight, and that had been a disaster. They were yelling and chanting, "Hit him! Hit him!" So, I did, and then I hit him again and again. Then, I just let up because I felt bad; I wasn't a bad kid or at least I didn't think I was. But when I let up, he just took off running, and I was okay with that, but my friends took off after him, so I started back in on the chase.

He made it to his house, and he was home free, so he thought. Little did he know that his mom was like my dad. There we were in his yard, and his mom made him come out of the house to fight me. She was yelling and cussing at him like a sailor. Now, that was something completely new to me. I had never, ever in my life heard a parent cuss out their kid before, let alone cussing him out to fight someone. This made me not want to fight him even more; I felt so bad for him. Here I was miserable inside, an outsider and suicidal, but I could not even imagine how he must have felt. So, I was standing there watching him cry because he didn't want to leave the house, and she was cussing at him saying if he didn't leave the house, she would beat him herself. He finally came out where I was standing, and she made him fight me. He charged me, and the fight was back on. I ended up breaking his glasses, and I don't even think he landed a blow, but eventually his mom said that her son had had enough.

I will never forget that day as long as I live. It reminds me of the Adam Sandler movie *Billy Madison,* in which Sandler plays a son (Billy Madison) whose father owns a hotel chain. One of the characters has a "hit list" of people he plans to kill because they bullied him. In time, Billy realizes that he has been a jerk and calls the guy to apologize. As a result, the guy scratches Billy's name off the list. I always feared that John would pop up one day to take me out; maybe he is still out there and will read this. If he does, I want him to know that I am so very sorry. Middle school was hard enough, and then to add jerks like me to the mix just compounded the problem. After junior high, I never saw him again. I do pray he is well.

I hope that your elementary and junior high days were smoother than mine. I have devoted the whole next chapter to high school because it didn't all suck. Finally, right?!

CHAPTER 4

THE GLORY DAYS

Oh, the glory days! How many men and women relive their days in the sun—whether it be their high school days, college years, or any time? Heck, most of us men lie about our glory days to make us feel good about ourselves, LOL. Until I was about 24 years old, I definitely thought that my glory days were my high school years. That wasn't because I played sports; it was more because of the antics and chaos that I caused. It was just fun. When I was a youth pastor, I had to remind myself not to glamorize my glory days too much because I would have been sending the wrong message to the kids that God had entrusted me with. But that was hard because I had so much stinking fun. There were plenty of consequences for the bad times, but I did not care one little bit. For most of those years, I was intoxicated in one way or another, which is bad, but that was not why I had so much fun. The fun came from doing stupid stuff and the people that I did the stupid stuff with. The fact that I am still alive is proof positive there is a God because I should have been dead a million times over.

Freshman year of high school was a fresh start for so many, and for me and my mom, it was the fresh start she had been praying for. That fresh start lasted about 30 minutes! Guess what happens when you are a freshman over six feet tall, and your brother didn't have the best reputation at the same school. You get bullied, and you get it bad! Day one, seniors started hazing me. At lunch on the first day, I remember running for my life. I was like, "Man, this has to let up," but it didn't. I played football and tennis, so I knew that eventually, I was going to get it, but I wanted it on my terms. Usually, when you get hazed, it will happen once, and then they let it go. The keyword was *usually*. Not in my case. First week in tennis, they got us freshmen in the locker room bathrooms; they peed on the toilet seats and made us push a penny around with our noses, and then one of them would kick the toilet to make the penny fall in, and they would make us reach in and get it. Yeah, we all did it, or we knew from experience we would get beat up the whole school year. Did you see the movie *Dazed and Confused*? That movie was set in Texas in the '70s, and this was in the '80s, but trust me, the hazing hadn't change much from what they showed in the movie.

Football hazing was far worse—well, not at first, but it turned out to be worse in the end for me. I had made varsity as a freshman, which was a great thing, but the bad thing was I could not run from all the guys who had been trying to get me. So, there I was in the back of the bus coming home from an away game that we won, so everyone was in a good mood. They were even being nice to me, and they even said I was all right. But—and there is always a but! They said they were going to let me off easy on the hazing; all I would have to do was moon the car behind us, and that would be it. I was like, "Heck, yeah!" I had mooned lots of cars, so this would be great, and I would not have to worry about being hazed for the rest of the year. So, I did it, and everyone was laughing and patting me on the back and having a great time. Next thing I knew the car passed the bus, and we were stopping. I'm like, "This cannot be good." What I didn't realize was that at every sporting event, a member of the administration had to attend the game to represent the school, and at this game, the administrator happened to be the principal. So, I had just mooned the principal and his family. Yes, of course the guys knew this, and they apologized, but at least I would be left alone. So, the next Monday in homeroom, I was called to the office to receive my punishment, three days in the SAC class again—yes, the same one where I had spent more than a month the previous year, the same one our church deacon oversaw. My mom was embarrassed again because she was notified of my antics, of course, so I was in trouble at school and at home. Finally, I finished my three days, but instead of being sent back to my regular class, they sent me back to the principal's office.

I was completely baffled by this because I had done my time. Once inside the office, the principal started in on me and proceeded to tell me that if he had known I was such a pervert and degenerate, he would have expelled me for what I did. I was in tears because I had no idea what he was talking about. He then let me in on it; he said he reviewed my file and what I did to get into trouble the previous year. He wouldn't even let me defend myself but said if I did one more thing, I was done there. So, I was definitely walking on eggshells from then on because I was more on his radar.

Can you think of a better start to a school year? This all happened in the first month! Then, the typical grade slide happened because I still did not know what I was doing. I was absolutely clueless in English and math. Science and history were mostly about memorizing, so I was passing them; plus, I always enjoyed history, and science had that good-looking teacher. Unfortunately, I learned that the easier days of middle school were over. What made this school hard for me was this was the school that my sister and brother graduated from. On one hand, you have my brother who was bad, and on the other hand, you had my sister who was an angel. So, every teacher wondered which one was I like. They prejudged me and assumed that because I wasn't the student that my sister was, then I was automatically like my brother. I made it there almost a semester before my parents pulled me out, saving me from failing. This would be the first of seven high schools in four short years.

My second high school was a Christian school in the North Shore area, which was about six miles away. It was a small, very strict Independent Baptist school. Girls wore long hair and dresses, and for PE, they had to wear long shorts. It was weird! I had never seen anything like that, and let me tell you, that school was not ready for me. Because I was the new guy and outsider, I was a hit with the girls, and I made friends easily. But I quickly got on all the radars of the teachers and administration. It didn't help that one teacher's name was Mrs. Butts; I mean, come on; I was 14! That was just too easy; it was like a pitcher in the MLB throwing a beach ball to a hitter! But I did try my best to be good and learn, because at that school, I was a god among boys. I played every sport and was the star, and everyone loved me for what I brought to the table, at least athletically.

This was the school where I got my first girlfriend, but I messed that up because one girlfriend was not enough. I didn't even hold hands with either one of them, but I was so blown away with the fact that girls were actually showing me attention; it was just an overload, I think. Plus, the school had this rule about not even getting close to girls, like at all. I think it was the "leave room for Peter, Paul, and John" rule or something. Either way, it was a no-go, and honestly, I didn't care; I was having a blast! I also was gaining some good friends, George and Anthony. George was a rich Greek kid whose parents owned a local restaurant, and Anthony was a karate phenom from Philadelphia who had a cool Rocky Balboa accent. Every weekend was spent with these guys, and it was just adventure after adventure. This was the only time that I didn't touch a single drug or drop of alcohol; I think that was because I didn't want to influence them. These guys were the real deal to me, pure-like, and I didn't want to mess that up, and I didn't miss it or want drugs or alcohol when I was with them. One of the funniest and weirdest things that we did was make up stupid words and phrases, and that used to annoy the crap out of the teachers, not to mention our parents. I mean, every time we saw one another, we would say this one special phrase, and after we said it, we would just die laughing for some reason. I still remember the phrase, *Yip yip yome!* That's all it was, but to us it was funny as crap. We had so much influence on this school that it banned the phrase. I kid you not! My mom knew my time was coming to an end at the school when she dropped me off one morning and, as I was getting out of the car, there was a chorus of little kids screaming, "Yip yip yome!" I am smiling as I type this because this truly was a fun time for me; it was one of those rare times when I fit in, and that felt amazing. I miss that feeling.

Well, my time did come to an end at the school. That's kind of misleading. I finished the school year and was asked not to come back. Oh wait, is that the same thing? At least they let me finish the school year, and they passed me. So onward and upward, right? Next up, another Christian school in the next town over called Channelview. This school was at the other end of the spectrum. This was more of a charismatic church; girls wore makeup, regular shorts, and it was wild. This school was clearly full of kids who had been kicked out of public school! It was crazy there, and the teachers were clueless. Drugs and alcohol were back on the menu, but this time I was doing it just to fit in. I think it was the second day when I saw kids pouring a liquid substance into a can and huffing it in class all the while the teacher was in there. I mean before and after school on the property, we were all smoking cigarettes and other things. This school was also a big opportunity to shine as far as athletics went. Sadly, this school didn't play my old school, because I would have loved to put a smackdown on them.

I did meet some very good friends at this school, though, and then, through this one relationship, my first band was formed. My friend's name was Ishmael, and he was a big guy; whereas I was tall, he was portly. Do they still use that word? So even though I was a sports star at the school, the girls did not care one little bit about that like they did at the previous school, so I was back to being in my shell, so to speak. Ishmael, or Ish as I called him, was like that too, and what was odd was his parents were the polar opposite of him. His mom was a beauty queen, and his dad was an amateur body builder who shot up steroids in their bathroom. Yeah, he left it lying around along with their weed. They tried to get Ish to eat healthy and take care of himself, but he was into D&D and heavy metal. I liked the heavy metal but did not get the whole role-playing game stuff. Ish was learning how to play the bass and was getting good; he had a friend named Matthew who had a drum set, this kid who was the spitting image of Randy Rhoads and played like him too. For the life of me, I cannot remember Matthew's friend's name, but he also played a Flying V like his idol. Man, he was so good; I played rhythm guitar and was the lead singer. The crazy thing about me was that I lacked social skills and kept to myself, but I would be unfazed by the stage or being in front of people. We just performed at the school/church and at house shows. Man, those were crazy.

The odd thing I was starting to notice was that even though I was happy or having a great time, I still had dark moments periodically. They were increasing in frequency; it also didn't help that we became friends with some people who dabbled in the occult. Sometimes, I wonder if my memories of those particular times are real. I found Ish about 10 years ago on Facebook, and he confirmed that they were real. He stated that he was doing good and had a daughter who was his main focus. As soon as I found him, he quickly faded away. I think he was still using, and I am not about that life.

After one year at my new high school, some pretty important bonds were made, and some devastating paths were laid out too. As I said earlier, I am a people pleaser who will do anything to have friends, even to my own detriment and that of the ones I love. Ish was the same way; our metal scene was filled with fast girls, heavy drugs, and a lot of alcohol. I know what you are thinking, "But you both were only 15." This was the '80s, and our age did not matter; I could walk into almost any convenience store and buy beer, and if I couldn't buy it, we sure could have "wahoo'd" it. Back in those days, for some reason, when you stole beer, as you were running out the door, you would scream, "Wahoo!" I still have no idea why, but we did. Beer or Boone's Farm wine and "Mad Dog" 20/20 were a given for the weekend. Drugs would range from huffing different items such as weed, small amounts of cocaine, and gobs of acid. I loved doing acid; it truly was my escape, literally. Every weekend was the same, and since I was over at Ish's house, I didn't have to go to church on Sundays, which would have been mandatory at my house. So, I was a 15-year-old male with suicide ideations on a regular basis but partying like a rock star, funded by parents who never had a clue. I still went to Wednesday night youth group where I caused havoc. I remember one night, the youth went bowling in North Shore, and I must have been acting like a fool because our neighbor from across the street threw me up against the building and threatened me. He was one of the deacons; he was my nemesis's uncle. I just remember being shocked and thinking, "Like, wow, Mr. Holy Man!" I think he was thankful I never told anyone about that because he stayed away from me every time I came around.

I did fine that school year and wasn't even a discipline problem. Imagine that! However, I still won the class clown award; I couldn't pass up that coveted award. I also had a date with a very sweet girl for the school dance. My brother, who was home from the Marine Corps was our chauffeur. Okay, that was a crazy night! Somehow, we lost my brother somewhere, but I was driving my parents' car without a license all over downtown Houston—without incident, mind you, so not too shabby. But somewhere along the way, we picked up a 1981 white Corvette Stingray, and we all took turns driving it.

I still have no clue whose car that was. I also vaguely remember a Taco Bell on Montrose or Westheimer where we were being stupid inside and outside. There were about 14 of us from the dance. It was a fun night. The girl broke up with me because she didn't think I liked her. You know why? Because I didn't try anything on her! Ha-ha, my social awkwardness struck again, but it was for the good because later I found out she wasn't a good girl. See, when you grow up in a very strict religious home, you see people either as "good or bad." Or at least that is how I saw everyone. Or that is how I categorized girls.

One weekend, my routine was interrupted, and I do not like change; change is bad. My parents told me, "Hey, we're going to go to a place called Buffalo, TX." I am not sure how I responded, but I know that I went, and I had a blast! They say that Buffalo, TX, is "God's Country." It has rolling hills, beautiful wooded areas, and loads of wildlife. That happened to be where they were having their yearly event called the Buffalo Stampede, which is a huge fair-type event at the city park with games, square dancing, and lots of food. Oh, and lots of beautiful country girls! I had never seen so many beautiful girls in my life in one place. When they said God's Country, they weren't lying! I was walking around, and they had this dunk tank, so I decided to give it a try. It was probably $1 for three balls, and it was put on by the school's athletic department. I remember this because of what happened after I dunked the coach three straight times. One of the coaches came up to me and asked if I lived nearby as he had never seen me before. I said no that I lived in Houston, and he said, "Too bad because we sure would love for you play up here, 'cause with your size, you could probably start right away." Okay, for a kid who didn't feel that he fit in anywhere and was not even comfortable in his own skin to have these guys wanting to hang out with me and coach me, I was on cloud nine. I know this is going to sound bad, but I was like, "Houston, friends, who?" I was sold on Buffalo! But soon, the weekend was over, and it was back home.

Thankfully, it wasn't long till I got the news that Buffalo would be our new home! Oh, I was so excited and couldn't wait to get there. We moved during the summer and didn't waste any time getting me registered for school. While we were there, we saw the coaches from the jamboree, and they were excited to see me, and they gave us the information for two-a-days, which are the summer practices before school starts. Basically, they run you till everyone is puking all over the place, except on the practice field because you did not dare puke on coach's field as he would either make you do sprints or up-downs. In 100+ degree heat, I don't know which was worse, we will call it a tie. Okay, there is a huge downside to being the new guy and being a big guy. Everyone wants to see how tough you are. I'm proud to say that during my time in Buffalo, I only lost one fight, and that was to a girl. Yes, a girl. I was making fun of her boyfriend at football practice and razzing him because he was on defense and I was on offense, and I was getting the best of him. I made a joke about her, and he laughed because it was funny. We were friends, which made what happened next worse. Well, the joke got back to her, and I guess she did one of those, you better defend my honor things. He did, or he tried, and I was beating him up until people broke it up and pulled me off him. When they did, she came in and started punching me in the face. Yeah, I deserved it; it was a bad joke. So, her boyfriend and I were sent to the principal's office, but we were joking and laughing again because we both looked beat up. Then our coach showed up and literally beat our butts with a paddle, ouch!

The house we were renting was in the woods, and it was amazing. (I always thought we owned the house, but it wasn't till I was an adult that I found out different.) I mean, a kid could not ask for a better place to live; the property behind us had a pond that was stocked with bass and catfish. There were coyotes and panthers in the area. Deer were everywhere; our dog would chase them down and bring babies up to our doorstep as a gift, I guess. I know that's sad and horrible, but he was an amazing dog; his name was Charlie. We think he was just playing with them because he was very docile with everything—except with deer, apparently. The home was surrounded by woods that hadn't been developed yet, but the acreage had roads cut through it, so I could ride my bike and later drive my truck and explore through there.

Speaking of trucks leads me to one of my not so great moments. I had turned 16 in April that year, and my friend down the road and the one behind us were getting four-wheelers for Christmas. Their parents had already told them, so they knew what they were getting. Since all the roads around our house were dirt, a four-wheeler would just be the perfect thing, so I asked for one too just like my friends. Fast-forward to Christmas morning, I was so pumped and excited. My sister was home from college, and everyone was waiting for me to wake up because the big surprise was waiting for me outside. They were all waiting to see my face when I saw my gift! Boy, did I let them down. I looked outside expecting to see a four-wheeler, and there, technically, was a four-wheeler, but it was of a different sort. I saw it and went ballistic! I threw a huge fit, saying I didn't want it, saying take it back, because I wanted the four-wheeler of my dream! I am still ashamed of how I acted. My dad almost never cries, but I think he did that day. My Christmas present was a Ford truck, a custom painted truck with custom interior with sweet rims and a Boss 302 engine! Man, I wish I had that truck now; that's how cool it was. I remember when my friend James came over later that day and he was like, "Dude, you are an idiot; this is way better than a four-wheeler!" As I am typing a lot of this, it is scary how much Keegan is like me.

So, after my friend talked some sense into me, I had to go eat some serious crow and apologize to my parents and hope that they would still let me have it. In my defense, though, I never would have thought or dreamed of getting a truck or a car especially since I didn't even have a permit yet. But I was wrong, and back then, people would have called me spoiled. Now, looking at things through the lens of Keegan and all the research that I have done, I think that my reaction might have had more to do with things going undiagnosed. Thankfully, my parents gave me the keys and told me that I could only drive on the dirt roads around our house. That was enough for me, spinning tires, blaring music, and fishtailing off into the sunset!

While all this was happening, school was in full swing, and I was a junior, so this was an important year for me. I'm not saying the teachers passed me so I could play sports, but they passed me. This also was the first time I had ever heard of a teacher, a female teacher that is, having an affair with her students, and yes that is plural. She had a thing for her senior students even though she was married and had kids. During my junior year, one of this teacher's kids was riding his horse on a trail through the woods when a panther jumped from a tree and knocked him off and mauled the back end of his horse. After living there for almost two years, I had only seen one panther, and that was enough. We would hear them almost every night, though, not something you want to mess with.

My drug use had calmed down to only smoking pot because that was the only drug we could get our hands on, but the main thing was drinking. Man, those country kids could put away the alcohol. I wasn't even in the same ballpark as these people. The girls could drink me under the table. The big drink besides beer was Everclear because it was clear, hence the name, and it was odorless and tasteless. It was deadly, especially when mixed with something like pink lemonade. We would buy a large drink, pour half of it out, and then fill the bottle with alcohol. We would drink the mixture through a straw and then pray that we would wake up in the morning. Many mornings, I didn't even know how I got home or where I was, which is truly sad, but at the time, this was an every weekend occurrence. I don't know how my parents didn't know; I really don't know. I remember one party at a friend's home, which was a two-story; one of my friends fell off the loft area and crashed through a glass table, but the party kept going. The more this kept going, the less I was interested in sports and a lot of things.

I ran with two friends, James and Ricky. James was shy and awkward. Ricky was the bad kid who was always getting in trouble; he had been in trouble with the cops since junior high for things like vandalism and stealing. Everyone knew Ricky, and they all warned my parents about him, but he was such a nice kid they didn't mind me hanging out with him. Honestly, I never really saw Ricky do anything bad—well, not anything that we weren't doing, which included underage drinking and driving under the influence. I know that is horrible, and I would never say that it was okay or condone it. Some might be asking, "Where was the law enforcement?" Well, he was there; he would confiscate our beer or liquor and use it at his parties. It's the life of a small Texas town, I guess.

One of the biggest events during my time in this wonderful little Texas town was my first real, serious girlfriend. I took her to prom and everything. She was from another town, and she broke my heart by cheating on me. To this day, she still has this problem. I kid you not; I joke with her about it on Facebook; she says she doesn't know why she cannot be faithful.

Soon after the prom, we went out on a double date with my cousin and his girlfriend; both girls were on the drill team at the school. They were really sweet girls, and I wanted to kiss my date so bad, but I had no courage whatsoever. Finally, we got to the end of the date, and the girls were going into the house. My date looked back, ran back to me, and kissed me like I had never been kissed, smiled, and then ran into the house. I was over the moon! Wow, I might have been in love or something; I don't know, but that's how good of a kiss it was. A week later, she moved away. Are you kidding me? Ha-ha; they call me Job! My family didn't last too much longer in Buffalo, and then, it was back to Houston. Well, just north of Houston, to Spring, TX.

The summer of my senior year started off with a bang, seriously a bang right into a light pole. We were staying in a hotel while we looked for a place to live, and I took my truck and drove back to my old neighborhoods to see if I could find any of my old friends. No one was home from the C.E. King area; then I went to the North Shore area and said hi to a couple of friends from the first Christian school I attended. I saw my two buds, but they were busy that night and couldn't hang out. Then I drove about two miles to Ish's house and of course he was there—nothing against him, but I figured he would be there. So, I hung out with him that night for a while. It was great to see him and a couple of the other guys. No girls, ha-ha, but it's all good.

Later that night, I went back to the hotel and when I was driving through the hotel parking lot, I must have blacked out and hit a light pole that was encased in cement. Welcome back to Houston, Job! Seriously, though, it was a freaky thing to wake up with my truck wrecked and not even realize how it happened. You can imagine that I was freaking out, not to mention panicking about how I would explain this to my parents. Thankfully, I wasn't on anything for once in my life after spending time with Ish and my old friends. I know some of y'all must have been thinking that! I don't blame you; I would have questioned myself. But this incident started a long and frustrating stint with doctors and coaches at my new school. Coaches who were world class! The head coach at my new high school was the former head coach at Texas A&M; the defensive coordinator was a former lineman for the Seattle Seahawks. I mean it was so cool, and it was even cooler that these men wanted me to play for them. This rejuvenated my interest in football; of course, it helped that I was away from all the alcohol, and I was in a community where I didn't really know anyone. Spring, TX, is 30 to 45 minutes away from my old friends.

There was a huge new problem, though; the doctors didn't know why

I blacked out. So, I was going through a lot of tests, and that kept me out of two-a-days. The coaches wanted me there with the team, learning the system, and building relationships, which I would have been happy to do. But as time went on, the coaches became agitated that I was not able to dress out, as if it was my fault. By the end of the summer and beginning of school, I had to wear a heart monitor, and that shut them up. But honestly, I was done; my heart was done on an emotional level anyway. Once I was finally cleared to play, the season had started, but my chances of beating out someone who had been working out all summer were next to impossible, and this was my senior year. I just quit; I quit everything. I wasn't doing my schoolwork. I wasn't doing anything—except drugs and alcohol, again.

We had moved into a condominium complex, and I hooked up with the wrong kid. He was only one guy, but that was all it took. He had all the connections, and then I met the next set of bandmates through him as well. This guy was dying when I knew him, so his mom let him do whatever he wanted. She bought him drugs and alcohol; she felt that he should enjoy whatever time he had on this earth. I didn't know this until after I was no longer friends with him because he was a jerk, but he had a lot of friends; well, he had a lot of people who used him. Tragically, he died two years after high school.

With my new group of friends—and I honestly don't even know if I should call them friends—I had a problem, which was about to grow exponentially. You take someone who is socially awkward and suicidal even when he isn't even sad or depressed and introduce him into a world of drug dealing, witchcraft, and theistic Satan worship, there was bound to be major problems. Yes, what a wonderful world my parents were about to be in. It is very hard for me to write this next part, as I am ashamed and embarrassed by this stage of my life. Everything about me changed. I have purposefully stayed away from talking a lot about my spirituality in the previous chapters, but I think you can clearly see a trend here: Jon was moving further and further away from God. Here I was, brought up in a very strict Christian home, and at that point, my close friends were theistic Satan worshippers, and some of their parents were practicing witches. That is insane! On top of that, my friend's sister's boyfriend was a major drug dealer who later recruited all of us. So, all this was going on, and I was flunking big-time at my fifth high school, so I needed to be pulled out of that school because I could not fail my senior year—of all years. I mean, am I right?

I was super pumped for my sixth high school! It was my third Christian private school, and it was like the first one that I went to. The girls wore long hair, dresses, and skorts. That is not why I was pumped, ha-ha. I was pumped because they played sports against my old school! Here was my chance to get my revenge! But my name is Job. Well, I started school, and I knew a lot of the students because I had played against them, and of course they knew me, as I had scored 44 points in the championship and left them crying. So, the players were very happy to welcome me to their school. But like I said, my name is Job. They got my records from the fifth school, and they informed my parents and me that there was no chance of me graduating due to my transfer grades. But what I could do was to finish high school by correspondence and still play sports there. See, they wanted me to play there; that's all they were worried about. So, that's what we did. I got signed up with the American School in Lansing, IL. Now, here is where I am truly Job! The first day of basketball practice, I broke my ankle. Oh, my gosh; that was just unbelievable, but yet it is believable. I was devasted.

This schooling was ridiculous, and the fact that I was at home meant that I couldn't do it. I was too distracted by everything in the house. I mean, we had the game shows and soap operas. Not to mention where we lived had a fully stocked pond and nice pool. What ended up happening was my sister and mom did my schoolwork. There, I said it. They did the work, and I cheated and did not honestly earn my high school diploma. My whole school career was full of me cheating and people covering for me. When I graduated from high school, I could not properly put a sentence together—it was literally that bad, and math was just as bad. I mean, how did I fall through the cracks?

How does one get into drug dealing? Simple, you get asked if you want to make some money. Remember, I love money. Mike was his name, and he dated my friend's sister. He was also one of the best drummers I have ever known. He asked me to sell the acid blotter paper. He asked Patrick and Joe to sell the weed while he took care of the cocaine. Here's a couple of quick stories for y'all. The first is the one that I was alluding to earlier about which I was so ashamed. I was at my house when I decided to take a hit of acid; it is such a bad idea to "trip" alone. To make matters worse, my parents and sister were home. So, I decided to take a bath. Oh, that was a horrible idea. I remember lying in the bathtub, and I was tripping hard, and I knew it was going really bad. It was going so bad I had to get out of the tub. I got dressed, and things went from bad to worse because apparently my dad said something to me, and I ended up cussing him out. It wasn't like, "Hey, leave me the f#*k alone!" It was way worse. When I was sober and they told me what I said, it shook me to my core. It still bothers me to this day. Let's just say I never did that again.

The other story is kind of funny, but it could have ended badly. One night, Patrick, Joe, and I were making a deal at a guy's house. The guy was huge, and I knew he ran with some bad guys. So, I was glad it wasn't my deal, but Joe and I were there; I was there because I had the truck. Patrick was known to pinch or take weed and replace it with I don't know what, a spice or something, ha-ha. Well, this guy wanted to smoke one with us before we left, but Patrick was antsy and was like, "No, we have to jet." Needless to say, the guy figured out that he was getting screwed over and pulled a gun on us, and shots were fired. The last story involves my brother, a host of other guys, and me on Halloween. Oh, and about 14 Harris County sheriff deputies were involved. Okay, we were drinking and driving around, smashing pumpkins, and I had brought some bottle rockets that I had left over from the Fourth of July. I don't remember who was shooting the fireworks out of the neighborhood, but they were firing off, and we were having such a blast. But you have to remember that my name is Job. Next thing we know, we see lights behind us following us out of the subdivision and as soon as we get on FM 1960, they turn on their lights and pull us over. Then, we hear, "Put your hands out of the window, and leave the vehicle one at a time." We had to walk backward and put our hands on the trunk of the car. We had 12 deputies with shotguns and pistols drawn on us! This was the real deal; if we moved wrong, we were done! They searched the car; they searched us and didn't find anything. Then, they asked us if were firing a gun in the subdivision, and we said no. Then, they asked if we were firing fireworks, and we said no. That's when we figured out that they were worried that we were doing a drive-by shooting. So, when they didn't find anything, they let us go. The weird thing was they didn't test us for alcohol or anything; I mean we had open containers and everything in the car, and they said nothing. We got so lucky that night.

So many times, I could have died and maybe should have died or been busted and have a criminal record. Looking back, it was God who shielded and protected me. I am crying as I type this because it reminds me of grace— God's grace and that I am so undeserving. Yet, He freely gives.

It gets darker before the dawn . . .

CHAPTER 5

IT GETS DARKER BEFORE THE DAWN

What if it stays dark all the time or most of the time? If so, then the time before the dawn is irrelevant. This chapter in my life should have been my happiest, and in some ways it was, but sadly there is always that but, and this one leads to my darkest hour to date. So, sit back as Job gains it all, loses it all, but does he ever gain it all back . . . ?

In 1994, I got out on my own; my parents had moved to Indiana where my dad's family lives and where I spent a lot of time during the summers. But I was 23 years of age and finally sober except for the occasional drink. From age 17 to 22, I probably couldn't have linked more than two days together without being high or drunk. I was always self-medicating. Not to mention that I was also dealing drugs, though I never got caught; without a doubt, someone was watching out for me. Some would say I was lucky, but if you look at my life as a whole, you know luck has nothing to do with ole Job here.

Well, I was massively screwed over by my brother in the apartment we were sharing in Houston. I was getting sued because my name was on the lease, so they were coming after me, but what could I do; he's my brother. I wanted to get out of the Houston area and start fresh; see, this is how it has always happened to me. My sister once said that opportunities just fall into my lap and then through no fault of my own, I lose them. Then, I'm left destitute and at the mercy of others to rescue me. So, I went to the Dallas area because I had family there, and I moved in with my cousin. His wife got me a job at a hardware store. Everything was great, I even got promoted; the owner liked me. I joined the softball team, and life was good. Ross Perot and other Dallas celebrities came into the store often and all was going well.

The company opened a new store in Grapevine, and I was offered the opportunity to transfer there. I took it because this was a great opportunity to advance in the company. I was there for a while and began making friends, and again, all was well. I was attracted to a girl; she was so nice, great personality, and attractive. But I am socially awkward, and I noticed that one of my new friends was also friends with her. So, on lunch break one day, I was sitting down with him when she came and sat at a table behind us. My back was to her, and her back was to mine. So, I quietly asked him if she was seeing anyone and if he would put in a good word for me. He said, "Oh you don't want to date her; she dates only . . . " I was like, "And so?" But whatever. We finished our lunch, and all was well. But they call me Job.

The next morning, I showed up to work. The employee entrance was around back and when you walked in you had to walk by the general manager's office. The general manager and I were tight; we always goofed around, and so when he stopped me in the hall and asked me to come in, I said what I always said to him, "What's up, boss man?" He told me that the girl I liked complained that I said that she only dated a certain type of guys. I told him that I would never say that and that I wasn't the one that said it. He said that they had already talked to the other guy, and he confirmed it was me who said it. Yep, fired right there on the spot. I was devastated; well, that was an understatement. I just walked out and cried in my car. I thought I was honestly going to retire there; that's how good I thought the company was.

To make things worse, I forgot to mention in all that story that I had gotten my own apartment and was living on my own. So, after feeling dejected, rejected, and betrayed by someone I thought was my friend, I went to the convenience store at the corner and got the newspaper to look for a new job. That's when I saw it: *Sporting Goods Store Needs a Team Sports Department Manager*; that position screamed me! I have played almost every team sport there is, so I rushed right over, and I was hired on the spot. It's like my sister says, "Things just fall in your lap." I loved working at this job because every day I got to relive my glory days and talk about sports! Not to mention that I was working in the Dallas area, and the Dallas sports teams did events at the local stores, where either players or cheerleaders would come out and sign autographs or whatnot. Jon in Dallas with the Dallas Cowboys equals heaven, ha-ha. I was there about four months before Job reared his ugly head. Our company was being bought out by an East Coast company. At first, we were told they were going to retain us all, but then they gave the entire store the axe including all management. They made that decision even though we had done all the labor of changing the entire store around for them—that was so nice of them. In a way, it was nice because we got paid for all that work. It was funny because people in the shoe department were stealing shoes left and right; it was a mess.

We were all unemployed; so, I had to decide what to do next. I tried to get another job, but I couldn't get a job to save my life; it was if all the doors had closed. So, I called my parents with a crazy idea. Wait till you hear this one: it's a doozy. When you are sitting in an apartment and it's just you, no friends, no distractions, all you do is think. You can think of some crazy things or remember some things that were said to you years prior. At this time, I was 6′ 6″ and 250 pounds and not into beauty and all that stuff. So, I was fearful that my request to my parents, especially my dad was going to be met with resistance. That is putting it mildly. I called them and spoke to my mom and said, "Hey, what if I move to Indiana, live with y'all, and go to cosmetology school." I waited for a laugh or some offhand comment, but her reply was, "Okay, sounds good." My dad was even cool with it! It was like it was ordained or something.

Oh yes, let me explain why I came up with this idea. When we, meaning my parents and I, were living in Spring, TX, together before they moved to Indiana, I met this kid from Texas City. He was rough around the edges, so rough that I actually caught him stealing from some of the apartments. But I kind of took him under my wings, so to speak. Well, I don't want to make it sound like I did anything, but his sister, Rosie, told me that "I saved her little brother's life." He was my best friend; we did everything together. But his sister was and still is a very successful hairstylist, educator, and salon and school owner for Paul Mitchell in Houston. It's funny because we all used to play tennis together at the complex where we lived, and she used to give me free haircuts before she became best friends with Mr. DeJoria. Well, Rosie would tell us that we should consider becoming hairstylists because men stylists make a lot of money, and we would laugh and tell her, "Heck, no." But when I was alone in my apartment, that is what came back to me.

I made it back to Indiana, and it was so great to be back with my parents, not to mention all my other relatives too. So many cool cousins and aunts and uncles that I have always looked up to and respected lived nearby. It just felt right, no other way to say it. The other nice thing was I didn't have to work or pay rent; they told me to concentrate on going to school, and they would take care of the rest. It was a true blessing to say the least. At the time, I didn't see it as a blessing; I was just like, "Heck, yeah!"

I got signed up at beauty school there in Kokomo, Indiana, and it was a surprisingly easy process; they sign you up for the maximum amount of money you can get without you fully understanding what is happening. Nonetheless, it was done; school started in the fall of 1994, and the looks and stares started. I was the only guy at the time, so everyone was pointing, and the rumors were going. Finally, one girl just came out and asked me if I was gay. I mean, this was two weeks in, but finally someone finally asked. I mean, I was intimidating with my size I guess, but I also thought I was still approachable. Since that was out of the closet, so to speak, I had to focus on the actual school because all the girls had the upper hand on me. I had never braided hair, curled hair, or did my friend's makeup. Plus, I am super competitive, and I wanted that #1 chair in the front of the salon portion of the school. There are some things that I cannot turn off, and competitiveness is one of them. So, I had to work harder than all the rest of them, and I did. The rumors and the cattiness never went away because it is what it is, I guess, but I never let it stop me from being me.

Cosmetology school was no joke, but it was fun. I had a blast, and I would let the girls do all kinds of crazy things to my hair. I think I had every color under the rainbow. My favorite was white hair and the tips done in blue; it looked killer. I had my share of girls who wanted to date me, and there were rumors, but that is what they were—just rumors. I only dated one, and she was the receptionist, and we only went out twice. I started in the fall of 1994 and you have to go until you get fifteen hundred hours and meet all the requirements; then you have to go before the state board and take the test and do everything with your model. So, I did the first semester or however they broke it down, and we were about ready to go out on the salon floor to do customers. Most students are nervous about going from working on mannequins or doll heads to styling real people, but I looked at it as, "Finally." That was the odd thing; I have never really gotten nervous or had stage fright—not that I crave the stage or the spotlight, because I don't, not even in the slightest. I would probably live in a monastery if I could. But I have a love for people; I want to please people, and I want to be loved. Here was my chance to be loved. At beauty school, that was easy because it was mainly little old ladies coming for their roller sets and conversation, and I could do that. But I found out that I couldn't scrub their heads very hard or hard enough when I washed their hair. They would always say, "Harder, harder. Are you even scrubbing my head?" But, after a few ladies, I learned to use my knuckles, and they loved that, and my clientele list started to grow. This also meant that my chair was moving closer to the front, which made me very excited.

Something else happened over the summer sessions that would also change my life, for the rest of my life. It was the introduction of the high school cosmetology program, which usually met at the school for the students' first year. For their final year, they would be at the beauty school after a certain class period was over. So, we had all these high school girls running around, and that meant more stares and questions about whether I was gay, ha-ha. At 24 years of age, I was not interested in these girls that way and paid them no mind, but I am friendly with everyone. One group of them thought I was so funny, and they would ask me and others for help, and I would oblige. Plus, we would all hang out in the break room and goof around; it was like a big family so to speak. But in this group was one girl who was very shy. She hardly said anything, and I couldn't tell whether she was Hispanic or Asian or what ethnicity she was. She was pregnant, and everyone looked out for her, and of course, as everyone's big brother, I did too. That's just how I am. But she would come to the school crying a lot or looking sad; she wouldn't talk about it, so I didn't intrude. As she got bigger, we all joked because it was harder for her to cut and do hair. I didn't see or talk to that group as much after I moved to the front area and became the #1 chair. Of course, this also meant that I would be graduating soon.

Graduation came and went, and it was state board time. For someone who doesn't get nervous, I was nervous like none other. Imagine 250 people in a hotel conference room all dressed in white and freaking out because this test would determine whether we would become hairstylists. My mom was my model, which didn't help because I was cussing and freaking out because I had cut her hair too short during the haircut part of the exam, and I was having to do this "state board roller set" thing, which has finger waves and a roller set in it. Dummy here just cut his model's hair too short, and the finger waves and the pin wheels or whatever they are called were not working, and I was thinking that I was done. So, I did what I could, and I told the person who was judging my work what happened, and she said it happens, and she passed me. I passed! I couldn't believe it.

After I got my official results and provisional license, I went out and interviewed in the Kokomo area, and a lot of salons wanted me because I had a good reputation from the school, and that was nice. One huge problem, I needed money now; I didn't have time to build up a clientele, so I took a position with a chain in Westfield, Indiana, which is a suburb of Indianapolis. I was doing really well; I was making almost a hundred bucks a day in tips, so I got an apartment in Noblesville, which was basically next door to Westfield, so I didn't have a long commute. But one night before I had moved to my new place, I was at the movie rental place with a friend I had gone to beauty school with, and we ran into the high schooler that was pregnant. Well, she wasn't pregnant anymore; she was there with her beautiful little daughter and her older sister. We stood there and talked for a minute; she told me that she would be graduating soon, and I said that she should check out where I worked because it could be good for her since she had the baby, and she could make money right away and get insurance. She said she would think about it, and we said good-bye.

In time, I began making a lot of money; my friend's sister was right about guy hairstylists. I would have people waiting for me when no one else in the salon was doing anything, but the chairs in the front area were full. The life of a hairstylist is a crazy one, though, and the partying lifestyle started to creep back in as everyone in the salon, including the manager, all partied together. We partied hard, and on the weekends, Lord help those first haircuts, ha-ha, because who knows how those turned out. One funny story. I was working with one of my regulars on one such occasion. I was cutting her hair, and I was going through it and it was all kinds of jacked up, and I was like, "Who cut your hair last?" She replied, "You did." It was an awkward moment, but she kept coming back, and it goes to show that, sometimes, it's more about the person cutting the hair than the haircut.

One day, someone from my old beauty school came in to interview for the receptionist job, so it was cool to see a familiar face. Then, the next week, there were two other familiar faces there for interviews for stylist positions. Yep, my friend who had the daughter, who was a bit emotional at school, and her friend came for interviews. They both were hired, and it was fun because it was like having a piece of the old school down there. Now, my friend who had the daughter was really good at doing hair; her mom was a hairstylist from Chicago, so it was in her blood I guess, ha-ha. But we became competitors; we competed on everything, tips, number of haircuts a day, how much retail was sold, and average time of haircuts. The computer kept track of all this, so it was easy to be competitive. Another stylist in the shop would invite us to party at her apartment a lot because she had kids and couldn't go out, so we would end up at her place because she was like the mom of the group. Well, she had a cousin, and I thought he was a cool guy because he was nothing to me. He was half white and half Korean just like my friend and coworker who had the daughter. Now, in that part of Indiana, that was a huge coincidence, so logically she would eventually want to pair these two up and matchmake.

Okay, when I said that I thought he was a cool guy, it was because he was a dude; it doesn't mean I would want him dating my sister or any friend of mine. He was a drug-using criminal who had several arrests for battery. So, when I heard that our mutual coworker was planning a party in a couple of weeks for them to meet, I was like, oh crap; I knew I had to do something. But what? I mean she was a cool girl and we got along, but she had a kid. I know that sounds horrible, but please remember I grew up in a strict Christian home, and I didn't think my mom would approve if I ever dated a girl with a kid, so I never even thought about it as an option for me. When the week of the party arrived, I heard our coworker talking to her about her cousin, how they had so much in common, and I was like, "I cannot let this happen." So that night, after work, I made my move. I said, "Hey, Michele, would you like to go out with me sometime?" Yes, that Michele and my wife Michele are one and the same.

Think for a second how many different things had to happen for me to end up in Indiana, in the same beauty school, and working in the same salon together. Bigger things are at work here, and you will see more, so stay tuned.

Our first date was with our coworker and her boyfriend and Alana at Denny's in Kokomo, Indiana. Michele and I both had the chicken fried steak. I was the first one to ever give Alana this, and she loved it and still does or did the last time that I talked to her. Alana was such a beautiful baby; she glowed and just melted my heart. I told Michele that I fell in love with Alana first because it was impossible not to. She just did that with everyone who came in contact with her.

After a while, Michele and I were getting serious, and I knew I was going to have to tell my mom about Alana, and I didn't know how she was going to react. I remember it was like the moment when I said, "I'm going to go to beauty school." So, I said it, and I got the same response, "So." I was blown away; I had misread this situation too. So, Michele and Alana met the folks, and it was just perfect; they loved them both. Several months went by, and in October 1996, I asked Michele to marry me; I proposed after work one night in the office, and she said yes. We got married on New Year's Eve that year; life moves quickly.

Here are some funny and embarrassing moments from right before the wedding and at the wedding from both sides of the wedding. First, my parents and I were meeting all Michele's Korean side of the family; this included her mom, stepdad, grandmother, and grandfather. Her grandfather had a prominent position in South Korea, so they were very dignified in how they acted; then, there is my dad, ha-ha. We were all sitting at this restaurant. Please try to remember that her family is Korean, not Japanese, not that it matters; you will realize this in a moment. So, we were talking about Asian food or something and my dad or I mentioned that he had taken my mom to Benihana once, and then Dad started mimicking the Teppanyaki chefs with a side of good ole stereotypical Japanese, Jerry Lewis–style impression.

Michele's family just sat there in silence, and I think I died a little that day. Now, Michele's dad loved it. He finally had a friend to make fun of her family with. The last story I will tell is about some of my dad's cousins at the wedding who were asking people loudly whether Michele's family were North or South Koreans. Well, you cannot choose your family, ha-ha. But the wedding went off almost without a hitch except for the fact that the photographer almost lost Michele's rings, and her uncle who did the ceremony forgot half the vows. No time for a honeymoon because this was a busy time for the salon. Still haven't had a honeymoon.

Michele and Alana moved into my apartment, and I was so excited because I had Alana's room all decorated as Disney's 101 Dalmatians, which was coming back out on VHS. Some of you may have to Google what VHS is, ha-ha; I'm old. We were a family, but we made some mistakes right off the bat. We had gotten a large chunk of change from the wedding gifts, and Michele thought it would be a good idea if we took some time off work to just be a family and so that Alana could fully acclimate to me being around full time. See, she never knew her biological father; he had only seen her one time, and the one time he did see her, he brought the girl he cheated on Michele with. Now you understand why Michele was crying so much through beauty school. So, I was the only dad that Alana had ever known or ever called dad. I remember lying under her crib singing her to sleep. I would sing a variety of things: The ABC song, the numbers, a lot of Garth Brooks, and George Straight were her favorites. While I sang, she would hold my hand till she fell asleep. Those were the days when I was the most important man in her life. I remember the process of adopting her; man, that was a long one. They required that we take out an ad in the newspaper, inform her biological father's family of the adoption because he had to be notified in case he wanted to contest the adoption. So, he had all this time, his family knew, and nothing, not a peep from him. I was relieved of course, but I never understood how he could not want anything to do with his own daughter.

While we were still on break from work, we decided to go visit Michele's mom and family in Chicago for a few days. Now, we had a cat—a special cat. He loved straws; he would pull them out of your drink and run off with them, or you could place them somewhere high and he would jump up and grab them. Oh, and he could talk! I almost forgot; he would say, "Wa-wa" if he didn't have any water in his bowl, and he would also say, "Momma." Seriously, it was plain as day! But Michele's mom is highly allergic to cats, so we figured he would be okay in the apartment over the weekend with some extra food and water laid out. Well, while we were gone, the cat turned on the water faucet in the bathroom and flooded the bathroom! I'm not joking; they found out because the water started coming out under the front door, and the neighbor called the office. That's also how they found out we had a cat. Well, our time was through in that apartment, and we ended up living with my parents. That was fine for a while. Then, Michele's mom invited us to move to Chicago with them, but Michele wasn't very keen on the idea because they hadn't always had the best relationship or actually any relationship at all. That's a tale for Michele to tell if she so chooses. But I love new places, and I love big cities, and I pushed for it. So, we moved up there, and it was fine for a while. I was hired to manage a salon in the same chain I was working for in Indiana. During this time, though, Michele was not happy and wanted to move back to Indiana. She was miserable, and after talking to my parents and her dad, I agreed to move back.

They call me Job. When we got home, I tried to get a job back with the chain that we had worked for, and they wouldn't even talk to me. Come to find out, the owner of the Chicago salons had been coming down into this area visiting the schools and salons using my name and recruiting, and that is a big no-no. So, no matter what I said, I never got a shot back with them, so Michele and I moved over to another chain that just did haircuts; they were just super and not just great. Did you see what I did there? Things were great; I was moving up through management; Michele was pregnant with Greyson and worked as long as she could. It was a blast just doing haircuts, and the location where I worked was near downtown Indianapolis. I did haircuts for radio personalities and sport stars; yes, they came to a chain salon for a $10 haircut. Honestly, I was surprised too. They sort of called me Job there. I tripped and hurt my back there, and I can pinpoint that my back problems began there. But I had a baby coming, and I didn't have time to do the physical therapy that the doctor had prescribed. My back continued to hurt, but I dealt with it the best I could.

It Gets Darker before the Dawn

Greyson made his grand appearance! The funny thing about his birth was that I was a blubbering mess. I mean, I had been there with Alana since she was six months old, well technically before she was born, but Greyson was my first biological child. So, there I was weeping so hard that I couldn't even talk. I went out to tell my parents and Michele's dad about Greyson being born and being healthy, but they were freaking out because they saw me and thought something was wrong with him. I was just so in awe of God, at the miracle of the birth of my firstborn son. God is so good; I was so undeserving of such a perfect little healthy baby after all that I had done in my life. But we finally got to bring him home to our tiny little apartment, and no one was as happy and proud as Alana was of her little brother. She was always so helpful, so helpful that one time when Greyson was probably two weeks old and Michele had laid him on the couch while she went into the kitchen for something, Alana tried to pick him up and dropped him on the floor. Needless to say, she freaked out, we freaked out, but he was okay. We think he was okay, ha-ha. He's a great kid.

I was still doing hair and working as an assistant manager and trying to rise up through the ranks to get off the salon floor and into upper management. Every year, like in most industries, there are trade shows, and I always enjoyed going to the hair shows. One year, I went to a show in Indianapolis and met the owners of a new franchise that was opening. We talked about me coming in and interviewing for a position as manager of one of their new salons. Here is the kicker; their salons were in my home state of Texas! So, a few weeks later, my dad and I drove down, as he was going to be my model, so I could do my haircut on him and show them that I could cut hair. We drove down; the interview went great, the haircut turned out great, and I was hired on the spot. We headed back, packed up, and headed down to the state that I loved so much and could not wait for Michele to experience it for herself.

Finally, the Locke family were Texans! I was so excited! Just a reminder, Alana was two years old, and Greyson was just three months old. We got to our place that we rented; it was a single-wide trailer, located in this really neat wooded subdivision in Magnolia, TX. It was only about two years old, so it was supposed to be in really good shape, but they call me Job. We opened the door, and it was filled with roaches, roaches everywhere. It was infested!

We had just driven over a thousand miles; it was late, and we were tired, and we were devastated, just absolutely devastated. We immediately called the landlord, and she claimed she couldn't afford an exterminator and said she had already spent the money we had given her. So, my dad talked to her, and she found some money and got it taken care of and put us up in a hotel till it was acceptable. It took a couple of days because the roaches were even in the fridge and freezer. It was just horrible.

But the good news was that I was able to go to work; I wasn't able to do hair because my Indiana cosmetology license hadn't transferred directly to Texas, and so I would have to wait for it all to clear up. Either way, it was no big deal because Indiana requires more hours than Texas, so it was just a matter of sooner and not later. While I was at work, I was doing their training and basically doing receptionist work, but I was getting paid as a manager, so I wasn't complaining. The owners were complaining, though, but honestly there was nothing I could do. I had fallen through the cracks at the Texas State Board. Needless to say, they call me Job. The owners let me go because they couldn't keep paying me and not getting what they were paying me for. This was horrible news, of course. What was I going to do? Not to mention that my back was still bad, and I was using this position as a way to get off the salon floor. As a manager, I could work part-time off the floor, so it was going to be perfect. We had some money saved, so we were good for a little while. The owners and I were still hoping my license would come through in the meantime. But no doors opened; I applied everywhere, and no one would hire me. We were getting desperate, as money was getting low and that is when my cousin and his wife heard about what we were going through. Well, she was a manager at a fast-food restaurant, and she told me that if I was interested, she could get me a management position. She didn't have to tell me twice, so I jumped at the chance to work for the king.

Now, things were going pretty well to be honest; I was enjoying working there. They had me running around different locations learning from the various managers. All was good, but here is an odd thing or at least I thought it was odd. Behind the counters, there were no chairs, not in the break area or even in the manager's office. You are to stand while you are on the clock. When you have a bad back, standing and rushing around for 12 to 14 hours a day takes a toll on your body. After days and weeks in this job, my body started shutting down on me. I couldn't get out of the car after work when I got home. I would have to sit in the car and rest for a while till my back would loosen up a bit before I could attempt to get out of the car. Then, to get out of the car, I would have to roll out onto my knees, wait there for a few minutes, and gain my strength up to climb up the side of the car until I was upright. Well, as upright as I could possibly be. Because my shifts were so long, I wasn't getting any time to heal, so I would get inside the house, shower, and go to bed, and then do it all over again. It was getting so bad at work that my back would just lock up and I would stand there crying at work. My coworkers felt so bad for me; the other managers would tell me that since I was new, they would just fire me if I couldn't do the job. The pressure of everything was so overwhelming. I had a young family that was counting on me, and I felt that I was letting them down.

So, I came up with a plan. For my whole life, I have been suicidal, even in the good times, which I never understood. I never had the courage to do it, but now I felt I had more than enough motivation to do it. I knew I couldn't go on with this pain, and I couldn't handle letting Michele and the kids down. Because I had so many friends in the area, I asked one of them for a gun, and they of course gladly obliged. Of course, they wouldn't have given it if they had known what my true purpose was. But I couldn't go through with it with Michele and the kids there; I wouldn't want them to see the aftermath. So, I came up with a plan and that was to get Michele to leave me—leave me and take the kids back to Indiana. I started being mean to her; I even started cussing at her and begging her to leave me because I had to quit my job. But she wouldn't leave; she refused to leave me! I begged and begged her to leave, but she wouldn't. So, I decided I was going to go through with my plan. Michele and the kids were in the living room, and I took the gun into the closet and locked the closet door. I have no idea why the closet door had a lock on it, but it did. But the main thing is that I knew that the door was locked! Here is another thing; Michele is not a Christian; she wasn't a believer; she did not grow up in a Christian home like I did. So, there I was; the door was locked, I was on my knees, weeping. I placed the gun in my mouth and pulled the trigger. It didn't go off; it jammed and to make things worse, the door opened, and Michele caught me in all my shame. The gun was still in my mouth, and she started to cry with me and says to me, "Just give it to God." Number one thing—that gun worked; I had firsthand knowledge of this. Second, that door was locked, and she just walked right in, and she isn't a Christian, but she told me to give it to God! Then she just held me and told me that it was going to be okay. Several days after this, my parents sent us money, and my brother and sister showed up to pack a moving van, and we were on our way back to Indiana. My parents have always done so much for us; I am so thankful for them.

So, we got back, and I started going to the doctor because my back was really bad. I started doing therapy and going to a pain clinic in Indianapolis. Because we were on Medicaid, I had to see medical students who were supervised by professors, which is fine except when I had to get epidurals. Oh, I remember one time this student was poking me, and my leg was moving, and I was twitching; it was bad—so bad that the professor had to step in and do the epidural. I felt bad for the student too. We laugh about it still to this day, but it wasn't very funny that day for sure. My back wasn't getting any better, and to make things worse, I was gaining weight like crazy because my activity level was next to none. We had been back in Indiana for a few months when we were invited to go to Chicago.

Maybe I wasn't the only Job in the family because Greyson has had some scares in his life, and the first one came when he was just 10 months old. This was the scene for a very nasty incident between me and Michele's mother and stepfather. Well, like I said, we were invited to take the children to Chicago to see Michele's Korean side of the family as they had not seen Greyson yet, and we were looking forward to the trip. Michele's family loved Greyson, and they passed him around and honestly it gave Michele a nice little break. On the third day, that is when tragedy struck. I was upstairs, and Michele and the kids were downstairs with her mother and stepfather. Her mother's home was a three-story townhome. They had placed Greyson in a walker, so he was enjoying zooming around on the wood floors, and then I heard a scream. I ran downstairs to find that Greyson had gone down a flight of stairs in the walker and he had blood coming out of his nose. Michele was freaking out, so I immediately took Greyson from her and took him upstairs and started to get ready to go to the hospital. I will be honest; I was furious that someone left the door to the downstairs open for Greyson to fall down. I was yelling and saying, "Where is the hospital? Where is the ER?" We didn't know our way around Chicago. They wouldn't tell me; they immediately took Michele off to the side and was telling her that Greyson would be okay and that we should just wait and see. I was like, oh heck no; that's not the language that I used, but I was livid that they were keeping my son from getting help. So, then they told Michele that they would take Michele and Greyson to their doctor. Michele was torn and didn't know what to do and just went with them despite my pleading with her that he needed to go to the ER. About 40 minutes later, they came back to the house; I already had all the bags packed, but they said their doctors said that he should have been taken to the ER. So, we followed them to the ER, and after they gave him the clean bill of health, we headed home. On the way out of town, we stopped by to say good-bye to her aunts and uncles, and her aunt made a strange comment before we left. She said, "So, she didn't get her." We honestly didn't know what it meant at the time.

We thought the drama of our Chicago trip was over, but we were notified that even before we had even left the city limits, her mother had started making phone calls to Michele's dad and to others saying that she was afraid that I was abusing her. Sadly, it didn't stop there. Once we were home, we went to an apartment complex to see about moving there. Michele went inside to get the application and Alana, Greyson, and I stayed in the car. Now, let me explain something about Alana; she was not your normal child; she was an extremely bright child with a large vocabulary for a two-year-old. So, while Michele went inside Alana asked me what Michele went inside to do. I replied, "To get an application." To which she asked, "So she can get a job and leave you?" When I asked her who she had heard say that, she replied, "Grandma Jeanie." Once Michele got back in the car, I let her know what happened, and Alana repeated it to her, and that was the straw that broke the camel's back. This is when Michele and I decided that our family comes first no matter what our family thought or said.

Sometimes, life becomes clearer when you decide to answer the call . . .

CHAPTER 6

ANSWERING THE CALL

This next part of my life and my family's life goes back to my childhood and jumps around a bit like flashbacks until it gets back to where the last chapter left off. As I stated earlier, I grew up in a strict Christian home and went to church every time the doors were open. We went whether we wanted to or not. I'm sure that some of you can relate. I also mentioned that my parents were a part of a new church plant. Our family was one of the founding families that stepped out of another church and met in a small place called the Pit Stop for a while. But the church grew and grew until we had a very nice building near a new subdivision adjacent to C.E. King High School and Elementary, so the church was in a prime location to attract families.

The church grew fast, and it was a very exciting time. Of course, my dad was a truck driver, so he was gone a lot. My mom felt a calling in her life when she was younger to be a missionary but did not heed that call. I think she still regrets that decision on some level. Well, her way of giving back and helping this budding new church was to be its janitor; it was a ministry for her. Perhaps, that was her way of making up for not going on the mission field.

We kids would go the church and help—or help by staying out of her way, in my case. But I remember that when I was around eight years old, I felt drawn to the pulpit and drawn to the pastor that we had at the time. I would sit in his office and ask him questions and talk with him. I would also stack hymnals behind the pulpit, stand on them, and preach fiery sermons. What's funny is I sounded like one of those great fiery black pastors from the South who would overemphasize words. Funny how I cannot remember what I had for dinner last night, but I can remember this as if it happened yesterday. I still remember the eight-year-old me standing behind that pulpit waving my arms and yelling out, "Turn or burn!" Because turn or burn was all the rage back in the day, ha-ha. The point is I felt at peace behind the pulpit, like I belonged. The pastor of our church was the one who got me to like the Dallas Cowboys, so he will always have a place in my heart. The odd thing is that he was only at our church for a very short time, but it seemed like he was there for years, but in a great way. Brother Paul Stephenson was his name; he left us and went on to do great things. But his leaving really hurt for a long time.

Sometimes, I would feel a gentle nudge that I was created for something that I didn't fully understand. But, at the same time, I was also feeling a lot of other emotions. I was one completely confused and out-of-control teenager. When I got away from my friends, drugs, and alcohol long enough, I would have moments of clarity. I would get these nudges again—sometimes at youth camp or outings. I mean the leaders must have thought I was a mess at these youth camps because I would be so broken and so open to God's calling and Him speaking to me, but when I got home, I would go back to my friends. The youth groups were not very deep theologically speaking, and so very few teens in my youth group were legitimately following Christ; it was hard to stay on that mountaintop. I know it sounds like I am blaming others for my lack of devotion, and I admit it; it was all on me. I would get back and after a few weeks, that mountaintop experience would slowly wane until it was nonexistent. It was a dilemma that many youth groups and churches faced in the '80s and still to this day. I think that it is even harder to hold young people's attention today because we have to entertain them, but that clearly is another book.

When I was 20 years old, I toured around with a Christian metal group, and they were a great influence on me. I spent so much time with them that I finally had a circle of friends that was good for me. I was back in church, not because I had to be but because I wanted to be. Once again, I felt the nudge, but I didn't know what it was, or what it meant except that I was supposed to work with teenagers. The cool thing was that teenagers in my area wanted to hear what God wanted me to say to them. But then they call me Job. Someone very close to me shut me down. She said that I was not qualified to talk to teens or anyone because I had not been to "school" and that my sister should take over. Well, the teens didn't want to hear from her; they saw her as a fraud. Teens can smell a fake a mile away, and once they tag you as a fake, you might as well be talking to a brick wall. Well, this was my first hurt by someone in the church, and it stung. It really stung, and, I let it push me away. Notice I took responsibility for falling away again because ultimately, we are the ones who hold the power, not anyone else. We are the ones who give the power to people for them to hurt us.

I ran from God after this with a vengeance; my drug and alcohol use were at such high levels that I can hardly believe I'm alive today. The things that I did during this period were downright reckless. Imagine snorting cocaine off the carpet because someone hit the tray it was on and spilled it on the floor; that is pathetic. But that was me. Imagine using so much LSD that you are not with it for days, and one of your friends ends up in the hospital because she burned her arm and face huffing off an air conditioner unit because she wanted to intensify her trip. Or dealing drugs and trading drugs for sexual favors because you have lost your moral compass. All the time, I should have died or been busted by law enforcement, but I made it through without any visible scars. Let me be clear; there are plenty of scars; they just aren't visible. Then, I recall the time when I was on my knees with a gun in my mouth and the gun malfunctioned; the lock on the closet door malfunctioned, and Michele caught me in all my shame and said, "Give it all to God!"

Give it all to God is what I did. See, giving it all to God means total surrender. That's also when true salvation is found—when we give all of ourselves to Him, when we finally come to the realization that there is absolutely nothing that we can do to make ourselves good enough to get into heaven. The realization that we need a savior—someone who paid the ultimate price—someone who laid down their life for me, for all of us. There is one who did that for us, and His name is Jesus. He was the perfect sacrifice, the one without blemish, the one who laid down His crown so that He could be nailed to a cross to carry a burden that wasn't His but one that He knew that I couldn't bear.

Jesus said, "Greater love has no one than this: to lay down one's life for one's friends" (John 15:13). How beautiful is that? I mean, I would lay down my life for my family and friends, but what about someone I have never met or for an enemy? The act of atonement is such a beautiful thing that the human mind cannot adequately grasp it.

So, where was I? A lot of the time, I was like a squirrel that had to stay focused, or I would chase rabbits all day. We moved from Chicago back to Indiana, as I said in the last chapter, and unfortunate things happened with Michele's family in Chicago, but hey, you move on. Onward and upward. I needed some time with God; I had accepted that it was God who had seen me through all the mess and mire and that He was faithful. This is what I did: I grabbed a tent, sleeping bag, Bible, notepad, and water and headed off to be one with God at the Mississinewa Reservoir.

(They call me Job. . . . I kid you not, as I was typing this on the front porch, a very nice lady came up and told me that the house we are renting just foreclosed. I am dead serious! Wow, now I have to go tell the family our options. I will be back.)

Okay, I am back. There I was in my tent at the Mississinewa Reservoir, in the summer no less, with no food, sleeping on the ground with a bad back, and trying to mend a relationship I had messed up. See, everyone thinks God leaves us or that He is distant. No, we are the ones who leave him; it is our sin that causes the distance or miscommunication to happen. Anyhow, there I was, and it was awesome; I was fasting and communing with God, and it was deep. Deeper than I had ever experienced before—so deep that it was scary, ha-ha, but scary in a good way. Because I felt God was saying, "Go to school, learn, and become a pastor." I was like, "Okay cool, a pastor!" I can do that. God said, "No, Jon, you're not listening. I said go to school first!" I was like, "God, I can't do that; you know, I can't do that, man." And this is where the really, scary cool started happening. God kept sending confirmation through scripture after every time we would battle this calling out in prayer. This went on and on till finally I was like, "Okay, you win, I surrender." It was like Jacob wrestling with the angel or Jesus because this isn't a theological discussion, ha-ha; but I already had a huge limp from my bad back.

There was one huge problem, though. I still didn't know what the heck to do, because first, I could barely put a sentence together; remember, I cheated my way through school. Second, I had no clue how this whole "calling" to be a preacher thing worked. Let me explain this calling thing in my terms— in basic layperson terms. A call on one's life is something you feel, backed by prayer and scripture and also backed by your life experience as it points toward your calling. A call should also be confirmed by the local church body, confirming that they see something in your life that reflects what is spelled out in the New Testament. I went to our church and talked with our pastor and told him what God was laying on my heart; he prayed with me and asked, "When do you want to preach?" I was like, "Wait, what?" He said, "This way, the church body can confirm if indeed you are in fact called to preach." So, he let me preach on a Sunday night when the crowd wasn't so big, and if I messed up, it wouldn't be that big of a deal, I guess. I had about two weeks to prepare, and this was before I had a computer or commentaries and all that fancy stuff to help me. I basically just prayed and had my Bible and pen and paper. For the second time in my life, I was really nervous, and I don't normally get nervous. But this was serious. I mean, have you read what the Bible says about rightly dividing the Word? This wasn't no joke. I went to the church during the week to practice and time myself and all of that. I had it down to about 45 minutes, and so I was ready to go when Sunday came around. When that night hit, I was sweating like a pig at a BBQ! I just remember praying, "God you know that I am not qualified or good enough to be your spokesman. I need you to intercede because without you, I am nothing. Amen." So, I stood up, and next thing you know I was done, and people were telling me what a great job I did. The funny thing is, I don't remember one thing I said or did, as it was not me; I can honestly say that it was the Holy Spirit moving through me that night. Not because I was something special but because I was a weak and broken vessel surrendered to His Will. Long story short, the deacons and the pastor felt that I was in fact called to be a pastor.

The next question was where in the world should I go to school? Now, I will not disclose what denomination I am because I will say some things later in this book that might paint some institutions in a bad light, and I don't want to do that. It isn't my intentions to do that, but it is my story. We checked out our denomination's website to see whether they had any colleges and seminaries, and we found two schools in pretty close proximity to where we lived in Indiana. We learned that all the schools had colleges connected with their seminaries, so a person could graduate from one and go right into the next. They had special times when applicants could visit the schools and stay for free—basically, a free vacation. Remember that we had never had a honeymoon or a vacation since we got married, so these trips were very needed for many reasons.

The first trip was to visit a school close by, and luckily for us, it coincided with their family weekend, so it was filled with games and what I call "Jesus chicken," you know, the yummy chicken place that is closed on Sundays. The only downside was that I was in excruciating pain the entire trip and could not walk very far without stopping. The next problem was that when I went to the classroom visits, they kept talking about the "rigor" of the schoolwork, which was scary to me for obvious reasons. However, that school's assistant dean said, "We are going to take you to the edge of the cliff and drop you off, and before you hit the bottom, we will grab you by the belt strap and pull you back up and then do it again the next day." That was the moment when I knew that school was not for me. The campus was beautiful; everyone was so very nice, and the city was amazing, but I knew that given where I was academically, this would have been way too much. I could not afford to waste money or to fail; these schools did not take grants or loans, and I didn't want to let my family down again. The memory of Michele finding me in that closet was still very fresh. Not to mention that I had never told anyone that I had cheated all the way through school. The first visit ended, and we went on to the next.

The second school was a couple of states away and, if you have ever had a bad back, you know that driving hurts and hurts a lot. We did a lot of stops so that I could get out and walk and stretch to get some relief. In the distance, we saw a green rectangular sign. At first, it was blurry and as we got closer, it became clearer, and finally, we read, "Now entering _____" city. But get this, as we passed this sign, all the pain in my back left! I had absolutely no pain. Not long before, I had been suffering to the point of sticking a gun in my mouth to end it all, and then we drove past this road sign, and I had zero pain. Why hadn't I come to this city sooner, ha-ha? We got to the school's admissions office to find out where we needed to go and still no pain. I was like, "Wow, this is pretty cool." But then they told us that where we would be sleeping was about a half mile away, and we had to walk there. Now, I hadn't walked a half mile in a very long time, but I also hadn't been pain-free in a long time, so I was up for anything. Michele was very concerned about me walking, as she didn't want me being laid up the whole weekend and unable to see the school and whatnot. But I didn't have much of a choice but to walk, and I wasn't going to embarrass myself by drawing more attention to my 400-pound body. The walk was actually a nice one, and I made it to the guesthouse still pain-free, to our surprise. The first night, there was just a casual one because check-in was from 4:00 p.m. to 6:00 p.m. They had nice sub sandwiches laid out for us to eat, and the next morning, we would start the grand tour of the campus and housing. One thing about bad backs that you may not know is that you do not sleep well because every time you move, the pain wakes you up. So, I hadn't slept well in about a year, and as I checked out the mattress, I wasn't optimistic about getting a good night's sleep. We went to bed, and the next thing I knew, it was morning! I slept through the whole night, no waking up with pain! It was unbelievable. I was praising God because there was no other explanation. It was the first good night's sleep I'd had in over a year; that place was too good to be true.

We started the day with a beautiful breakfast in a 100-year-old mansion that was part of the school grounds; then, we were off on an all-day walking tour of the beautiful campus. Yes, I said walking. I know that God said, "Do not test the Lord God!" and this walking was sure going to be quizzing, testing, and giving him a final exam because my back was so bad that I could literally turn the water on or off in the sink and end up being laid up for a week. It was that bad. That is no exaggeration. But I made it; day two was in the books, and still no pain! What in the world was going on here? Or should I say, "other worldly"? We had a great time that day meeting professors, and there was no talk of being thrown off cliffs—just the opposite. There was talk of walking alongside where each student was because they understood that some students would be coming right out of high school and others would be in their 50s and beyond. It was very comforting. Day three started with breakfast; then we went to see the different housing options; this was the conclusion of the school's tour, and we had to head back home. So, we loaded up the car and we were heading out of town, still pain-free. Then, I saw that same sign we passed coming into town. But this time, the sign read, "Leaving _____" city, and the moment we passed that sign, all my pain came back. I kid you not, and it came back with a vengeance. We took this as a confirmation of where we needed to be. Later that week, we found out that I was accepted into the program at that college.

Before we could finalize my plans to enroll in school, we had to settle my claim for social security disability. I have to say that life had not been a bed of roses; I had been turned down twice by social security disability and was awaiting a hearing with a judge, so that was scary. I had never been before a judge, and I didn't really know what to expect. We were broke and living off the charity of mostly my parents, as we were living with them. I was preaching more frequently and also teaching a senior adult Sunday school class. Now, that was fun and challenging because most of them had been Christians their whole lives, and they had at least some preconceived notions of what the scripture means. So, we would have some spirited debate at times, but it was always fun, and I truly enjoyed that season in my life. One thing that I didn't appreciate was that some members were feeling me out to see whether I wanted to be the pastor of that church because there was a faction that was unhappy with the current pastor. This would be the first of many things that I would not understand about the church and all Christianity for that matter.

The time came for my disability hearing in Indianapolis, and Michele and I were so scared. You hear that they always deny you twice and then you will get it, but that is not something you can bank on, especially when you have two small children. I remember being in a room with Michele and the judge and other individuals, and my chances weren't looking good. Finally, the judge looked at me and said, "Mr. Locke, tell me why I should find in your favor." I looked him in the eyes and said, "Sir, my family, my wife and kids mean more to me than anything, and I would do anything to provide for them. I would dig ditches for them if I could; I would do anything; you name it, and I would do it." He looked at Michele and me and said, "You know what, I do believe you, and I find in your favor."

Such a heavy load was taken off my shoulders, but there was one issue.

Remember, my name is Job. The lady who did the estimate for my social security wrote down the wrong dollar amount that I would receive every month. She wrote down $1,416 a month, and we banked on that. With that much, Michele wouldn't have to work, and I could go to school full-time—a decision we had been leaving for the following month. So, we were awarded social security disability and leaving for school within a month. This was November 1999; Alana was almost four, and Greyson was almost two. When we got to the school, we received our first social security deposit—it was only $416. There must be some kind of mistake! We were missing $1,000! Unfortunately, we learned that there was no mistake. Michele would have to get a job, and my mom was going to live with us and watch the kids for us. So much for finally being back on our own again.

Michele began cutting hair at the same chain we had originally worked for in Indiana as her name was not tarnished. She was and is a very talented hairstylist who quickly worked her way into managing three salons, sadly for no extra money. But the owners became like family to us and really took good care of Michele and us even after she no longer worked for them. This was a hard time for Michele as it was the start of a very long time that she spent away from the kids, especially at such young ages. At the time, I did not know that she did not want to be at work and away from the kids. She was always so positive and so willing to do whatever was needed for the family even if it meant putting aside her needs and desires. It breaks my heart for many reasons because I truly believe that Michele's current struggles most likely started back then. Michele's whole life has been put on the back burner, and I witnessed firsthand how her family treated her, and I never wanted to do this to her. So, she remained quiet about how she was missing out on the kids and me; like a good soldier, she kept marching along.

Michele wasn't the only one making a sacrifice for us to be there. My mom was living with us, watching the kids while I was at school and Michele was at work, not to mention cooking and cleaning as well. That takes a toll on your body and every aspect of you, emotionally, mentally, and spiritually. My mom was missing my dad, her friends, and her church back in Indiana. It was too much. Things were being said, and feelings were being hurt, but she was stuck because we needed her there, which only compounded the problems.

Finally, we had a major flareup. This was a flareup that should have come many years earlier because it was something that I had held against my mom for many years. Everyone in the immediate family knew that my mom had quite a sharp tongue and would lash out from time to time. In one incident years ago, she made a comment about my weight getting out of control, saying that I was going to die, and because of my size I wouldn't fit in a casket and would have to be buried in a piano case. Now, as a teenager who was struggling with so many different things, this comment hurt, and it hurt bad. I mean, my mom was all I had growing up, so this was devastating. So, all these years later, there was a blowup one night, and I let it all out and let her have it; she was completely blindsided. The damnedest thing was she had the audacity to say that she didn't even remember saying it. I mean this had been eating me away like cancer, ruined our relationship for so many years, and she didn't even remember saying it. That killed me all over again, and by this time, if I did die, I would in fact have had to be buried in a piano case, I'm sure.

This was easily the second lowest point in my life, and it signaled the end of my mom living with us. Now we would have to find day care for the kids. I have purposefully saved describing how my first semester of school went for the next chapter, but for the sake of this chapter, I'll just say that it was summer, and I was able to watch the kids. But school would be starting soon, and we were able to get day care at a local place that was recommended by a lot of the seminary families. But they call me Job. Alana was four and a half, and Greyson was two and a half. It's always easy to remember their ages and the number of years we have been married because they are two years and two days apart. For our anniversary, you subtract one from Alana's age; plus, our anniversary is on New Year's Eve, and there's no forgetting that. Greyson was not talking yet; they said that it was because Alana was talking for him. That made sense, but looking back and knowing what we now know, his delay could have been more than just that simple explanation.

I wish this story was a happy one, but remember what my name is. The kids had never been to a day care; they had always been watched by someone they knew and were comfortable with. So understandably, there was some adjustment for them, but it didn't take very long. The kids loved going; they couldn't wait to get out of their car seats to get in. But after a while, Greyson started fighting us when it was time to go in. He wasn't verbal, so he couldn't tell us, so we kept taking him, and Alana was still happy going, so we just thought it was a phase. One day it was really bad, and Michele was with us as I was going to drop her off next before going to school. Greyson's crying started at home; he cried all the way to the school and did not want to get out of his car seat; it was bad. So, we were trying to communicate with a nonverbal toddler on why he didn't want to go to day care anymore. Well, you know what, kids will surprise you. We asked him why he didn't want to go in, it was just that simple. He simply pointed to the building and pinched his arm. I was beside myself, and I asked him, "Greyson, is someone hurting you in there?" He nodded his head and pointed at the building again and pinched his arm. Let's recap: I am 6′6″ and 400 pounds, and someone was possibly abusing my toddler; this was not going to end well. Michele was bawling, and I was furious. We grabbed the kids, and she didn't want to go in, and I was like, "Oh hell, no!" I went in and demanded to see the owner or whoever was in charge, and I was loud. I explained what was happening, and they pulled up the names of Greyson's teachers. Get this crap! One of the teachers' aides admitted to it! I could have killed her, and it got worse. This was before we stopped saying the "R" word, of course. She stated that because he didn't talk, she thought he was retarded and that was her way of punishing him or treating him. When I heard that, I thought I was going to destroy the whole building with her in it. Then, Michele said to me, "Remember where you go to school and who you represent." When she said that, I grabbed both my kids, and we left and had a family day. She called in from work, and I didn't go to school. The worst side effect from this was that Greyson distrusted every black person that he came in contact with. He literally would cringe and cry; it took many years and one special friend of mine who invested himself in Greyson and, over time, all was good. But to this day, when I think of this incident and as I type this, I cry over this—that someone used their power and influence over one of my children in that way.

Answered the call, and now the revelation, and it won't be what you are thinking of!

CHAPTER 7

THE REVELATIONS JUST KEPT COMING!

I have to preface this chapter by saying that I was a blank slate when it came to theological terms, or anything biblical for that matter. I did not have a firm grasp on the trinity if we are being honest here, ha-ha. The school that I attended was a serious theological college and seminary with people who became missionaries, professors, and pastors. They do not offer a liberal arts degree and no underwater basket weaving classes. Some of the professors in the college were the seminary professors who required the same level of academic rigor from the students. Remember, however, I was barely able to put a sentence together, but I knew one thing. God had called me to be there, and if He called me there, He would make a way for even me to make it. I'm not saying that I am anything special, but for me to go to school reminded me of a lot of the disciples. Before you throw the book down and start screaming, "Heresy!" stay with me for a second. Many of the disciples were very normal guys who did amazing things because of what God did through them. My going to school and hopefully graduating would require Him to basically part the Red Sea again.

I remember getting syllabuses the first day; that was overwhelming because I had never seen one before. Especially when you see the course schedule and what and when all the assignments are due. My anxiety was already building up. Then, we went to chapel for Convocation. We did chapel three times a week, and they brought in big-time pastors that I had only seen on television or on the covers of books, and here I was going to get to meet them. Some of my professors were actually pretty big-time themselves, especially our school's president. To be in chapel with all those other students was a feeling like I had never experienced except maybe like at a revival, and chapel was held three days a week, truly a blessing. I still have the Bible that I used from those days, and the notes and dates with the names of the speakers, and it brings back many great memories. One of my favorite speakers was the late Dr. Adrian Rogers; he was such a nice man. He actually sat down and had a brief conversation with me. Dr. David Jeremiah was very nice as well; some of the speakers would even hang out on campus with the students for the whole day, and you would see them around campus.

Classwork didn't start till the second week of school as the professors gave time for everyone to get their books and get situated. Then, they hit the floor running, and I immediately tried to resort back to the class clown routine because that was my self-defense mechanism. This was met with mixed reviews—loved by the students and even by some of the professors. The only professors who didn't enjoy it were the ones who thought I was stealing their thunder or that I was funnier than they were. Thankfully, I had an English class, and I had to humble myself and go to the professor after class and explain my situation; she completely understood and said that she would help me. She was an amazing teacher; she also had some crazy beliefs that had people in stitches. I actually wrote a song about it called "Nephilim." It was a thrash metal song, and she allowed me to bring in my guitar and amp and sing and play it for the class. It was awesome. One of the most amazing things that I learned from her was that before she got her position there, she was a janitor. She has a PhD and two master's degrees, and she was a janitor. Her husband had been relocated, and they had two children in college, so they needed her to work. At the time, the only job that she could get in a pinch was a janitor's position. Every night, she would be taking out the trash and mopping. When she found herself getting bitter, she would start to pray, and 1 Corinthians 10:31 came to her mind; she said that she felt ashamed that she became bitter because God in fact did supply her with that job. So, from that point on she said, "I pushed that broom for the glory to God; I took out the trash for the glory to God, and I cleaned that toilet for the glory to God."

It wasn't long after her heart change before she was hired by our school as a faculty member.

All my teachers were amazing; I loved listening to them, granted I had no idea what the heck they were talking about, but it was awesome. I mean they spoke with passion and conviction, and I was in awe as I had never seen anything like this before. Plus, they would even argue with students! This wasn't even the most bizarre thing that I saw in my first two weeks of school. I saw fistfights between students! I was like, "What the heck! This is a Christian school and we're acting like heathens." Guess what they were fighting over. A girl? Nope. It was over some dude named John Calvin and the country Armenia. I was in shock, and I was disgusted by the behavior I saw. I saw not just one fight but several fights that first semester. I get that people are passionate; I get it, I totally do, but they were forgetting the main point. The point is that we are called Christians, which means "Christlike." Some of my friends were a part of some of these brawls, and I would just shake my head at them. It was like they wanted me to join in with them probably because of my size, but I told them, "I don't even know what y'all are fighting about." There were two guys who became close to me, and they are still my friends to this day, at least on social media. But I know if I needed them, I could count on them, and they could for sure count on me. I think because they were 18 and this was their first time away from home and me being 28, I was like an older brother to them or even a father figure. They were actually over at our place quite a lot, and the kids loved it when they were over. I loved it as well, but as far as "school" matters went, I relied on them as they relied on me for "life" matters.

Because Lord knows I was going to need help. As I was questioning God, I think others were questioning God on why I was there because I was so overwhelmed by the workload and this foreign language they were speaking. Come to find out it was called "Christianese," and it was something I didn't speak, read, or understand. I heard terms such as *tribulation, rapture, mid-trib, post-trib, pre-trib*, and a host of others that people got into fights over! It was insane! Everyone knew I was a blank slate, so they tried to sell me on their viewpoint, and even the professors would do this; it was baffling to me. One day in class, this hyper-Calvinist professor made some statements (yes, if you are a staunch believer in your viewpoint or hold a far-out version of your viewpoint, they will throw the word *hyper* in front of your name). So, this particular professor stated a position that made no sense to me; it was about how God predestined some to burn in hell and some not. Now again, this isn't a theological book, so I am not going to teach in it, but I encourage everyone to Google theological topics or take theology classes, as they are invaluable. So, me being a little smart butt, but also being completely ignorant on this subject because I didn't understand why a good and loving God would do something like that, I asked, "What about my kids?" Because I have kids and I was genuinely concerned about them, I wouldn't want them being predestined to burn in hell. The professor turned to me and said, "Don't worry, brother, because you have shown concern, your children aren't predestined." I was thinking, "That's some BS if I ever heard some." I called him on it, and he shot me down. It was a frustrating moment because in all the movies I've seen, students and professors have these awesome moments of debate; well, not here. I noticed that a lot of students saw what I saw, and it caused them to question. I do not think questioning is a bad thing especially when it leads to a deeper understanding of what you believe.

Being a blank slate can be bad, but it can also be a beautiful thing because God can speak to you in amazing ways without all the presuppositions that other students have. Even though I was much older than the other students, I was much younger spiritually speaking than they were. Now, I am not saying or even implying that I was getting a new revelation from God. I am just saying I was reading scripture under the guidance of the Holy Spirit without presuppositions. I wasn't reading it thinking, "Oh I'm supposed to read it this way because I am a Baptist or because I was raised this way." I was actually learning how to read the Bible properly; wait, that might sound bad to some. When I was a child in Sunday school or in youth group, people would talk about just reading chunks and chunks of the Bible. I was learning to dissect it verse by verse, praying over the text, and allowing the Holy Spirit to speak to me. Sometimes, I would read a chapter several times, or I wouldn't get past one verse because God would just blow me away! Every verse, every word you read seems brand-new when the Holy Spirit is illuminating it. The Word is truly alive! I had never been so alive either.

The Revelations Just Kept Coming!

My professors and some of the students also appreciated where I was coming from. I had two professors who used me as a sounding board, and we would sit and discuss various topics at great lengths because I would always seem to ask questions that they wouldn't think of and they would then be able to address them in whatever they were working on. Students would also come to me about theological things but also about life, which always made me feel good because I love to feel wanted and needed. I also came up with an amusing theory that a professor called the Lockian Theory, but the funniest thing was that I just recently saw on the news that someone else had a similar view that I had over 10 years ago. Now, this theory was basically this: when you are born, you have this innate knowledge, and as you get older, you lose it. I came up with this theory because of my observations as a parent; little babies just seem like they are so smart, and they read your mind and work it all out, but as they get older, they essentially get dumber, ha-ha. Not necessarily dumber so to speak, but they lose their innate knowledge. But when I first explained my theory, it was just hilarious, and it still is actually. It was during this time that this dark cloud had been lifted from my life. I was still in physical pain due to my back, but I was maintaining my weight because of walking the campus.

All that happened in the first couple of weeks of school, and the professors were warning us not to forget to look ahead for the research papers and other items that had deadlines. I was like, "Whatever; God's got me; He is going to see me through it!" Right? That's the saying, isn't it? What is a research paper anyway? Double space, single space, 10 pages, and who the heck is this Kate Turabian lady, anyway. I will tell you who Kate is; she is the DEVIL! I hate Kate with a passion! I still do not understand Turabian format, even with one of those squisher things that you can use to format your term paper.

Anyway, let's get back to my main problem. I am not a reader; I think the only book I had read at that point was *Where the Red Fern Grows*. Hey, that was a great book but nowhere near the caliber of what I would be reading. I was going to be dead meat because the school had us reading Plato, Socrates, and Aristotle. See, it was a seminary first, but to get accredited for the college or something, they had only one bachelor's degree, and it was in a discipline known as the History of Ideas. So, the required reading list was insanely tough, but by the end, you would be one heck of a scholar, and I loved that idea. I was someone who had cheated all the way through high school and then I would become a well-read scholar; that was so amazing. It was exciting to say the least because I was going to earn a degree in philosophy. I mean, can I get a "what, what!"?

I went to the only person I could and that was my English professor and begged for help, and she helped. She gave me some printouts and books that helped with reading books for the sole purpose for doing research papers and for writing research papers. I remember my first research papers looked as if the professors had "sacrificed a bull" as they called it due to all the red marks on them, but I read and reread every note they made on those papers, and I never made the same mistake twice. Eventually, my papers got better and better. I was passing, on my own, and I cannot tell you how that made me feel. Even now as I type, I well up with pride. God knew what He was doing, and He placed the right people in my path. I made it through freshman year I think mainly with Bs and Cs, and I was happy with that. It was a great first year of school for the student who could barely put a sentence together.

Summer break came, and that meant the kids and I were at home while Michele was at work. It was fun to spend the day with the kids; we took naps, watched cartoons, and ate snacks all day. It was funny because I would let the kids pick out their own clothes and when we would go pick up Michele at work, her coworkers would get a kick out of how the kids looked. Michele would smile and laugh but say that she felt she was missing out on the fun. So, we would try to make it fun for her when she would get home with family movie nights and a lot of eating out so she wouldn't have to cook.

We also went to Georgia that summer to visit her aunt and uncle who had moved from Chicago. That was a good trip until we got the pictures developed, and I could see how big I was. Why is it that you never see yourself as you really are, but as soon as you see that picture, it hits you? Not going to school for the summer took a toll. Not walking the campus every day and eating snacks all day put on the weight and really affected my weight and back problems in the worst way. Michele had been noticing that I was more and more restless during my sleep. My snoring was much worse, and I was catching my breath and having brief moments of not breathing. She used to say that she would just sit there and watch me to make sure I was going to start breathing again.

Fall semester came, and school started again. With this being my second year, the rigor was stepped up a notch, and I had to bring my A game. Unfortunately, I was waking up in the morning feeling like I had just fallen asleep, and I was exhausted when I got to school. I was falling asleep in class, and I stopped going to chapel so I could go to my next class and sleep at my desk and wake up when other students came in for class. So, I wasn't getting rest, and I wasn't getting the extra spiritual feeding that I had gotten the year before, and it was showing at home and school. The dark thoughts were back, grades were slipping, and I was yelling at Michele and the kids. It was just not good. If you can't rest, your body cannot heal. The school gave me the key to the elevator because I was having trouble walking up the stairs. This was embarrassing.

It was just too much. I finally went to the doctor, and he ordered a sleep study. If you haven't had one or know someone who has had one, just know this: they suck. The study usually lasts all night, and the worst part is they put these probes all over your head and body. They also videotape you, so needless to say, it is very hard to sleep with all the probes on you. They got me hooked up, and I was finally able to lie down, and they turned off the lights, and I was thinking to myself, "There is no way I am going to be able to fall asleep." They said that not only did I fall asleep but within the first 30 minutes, I had an "episode," which means I stopped breathing, so on came the lights. Obviously, I have sleep apnea, so they had to figure out how bad it was by putting a mask on me to push air into my mouth and help me breathe normally. My apnea level was the highest that my attendant had ever seen. So, I guess that meant I had it pretty bad. Well, I finally got my CPAP machine, and it was quite an adjustment, but the first night I slept the whole night through. I woke up refreshed and ready to take on the world! Everything changed, and everyone saw it. My professors didn't like the change for the most part because I was hyper, hyper-Jon. Ha-ha, did you see what I did with my name there? I am making new Christianese as I go. But home life, school life, and everything basically improved. It is amazing how sleep helps the mind, body, and spirit.

Remember, they call me Job. Regrettably, it wasn't always smooth sailing there. Michele had left the chain salon and begun working at a barber shop and was making much more money. I mean it wasn't even close, and she didn't have to manage three salons and worry about whether stylists were going to show up to work. So, this was a win-win for her and for our family. With this newfound wealth, we wanted to move out of seminary housing. The housing wasn't bad, but we could get a nicer place with more options for our family. We found a place, and this apartment complex was NICE! It had a pool and tennis court, and the inside of the apartments were very nice. Our neighbors who had been our friends in the seminary housing worked in the housing office and told us some things that we weren't supposed to know. For instance, they told us that they were replacing all the carpet with laminate and making some other nice upgrades in the kitchen. We informed the seminary housing office that we were moving out, and they gave us a move-out list, and we had the place clean just like it was when we moved in. We had the move-in checklist and checked all the things that were marked on it—things that were wrong with the apartment. So, we moved out and thought all was good. About a month later, we received a letter and bill in the mail for over $1,000. The housing office sent us a bill with a detailed list and surprisingly it was the same as our move-in checklist. I was very upset; I rushed down to the housing office and demanded to see the head of the housing office. I met with him, and he rudely talked with me how the apartment was so disgusting and showed me the video of the apartment, and I was just beside myself with anger. I mean, my mom and dad came from Indiana to help us clean the apartment and move us. This apartment was spotless, so I demanded to see our move-in checklist, and he called one of the workers to get our file and to our shock, guess what wasn't in there? Yep, that move-in checklist. Then, I said that I knew they were ripping out the carpet and had a contract with a local company already to do this, and he called me a liar even though you could see the company already working in our apartment and others replacing the counter with laminate. After several meetings with this man, he actually informed me that he has a black belt in Tae Kwon Do and that he taught soldiers in the Korean War; this was in the middle of a conversation with no reason for it unless it was some kind of veiled threat.

When I told the housing director about the flooring, our "friends" and neighbors claimed that I had made that up, and they never talked to us again. It is amazing that I supposedly made up very specific facts, but it is what it is. Things actually became very tense at school; the dean of the college refused to speak with me, and the president of the school refused to see me in regard to the housing department doing wrong toward the students. What is a person to think when the authorities "lose" documents out of files that were in their file cabinets, and the leaders refuse to even talk to me and others? It was a shame that this happened, especially when they claimed to have open-door policies. We got the bill down to $400, but after seeing how this man and this housing office treated us and others, I could not stay at this school, so I withdrew.

My whole life has been filled with events like this—for "principles' sake" quitting or leaving a situation no matter the consequence because it was a matter of principle. Did I pray about this or consult God in any way? The simple answer is no. Impulsivity has always been a problem for me, and how eerily similar to Keegan that is. I had heard of a school in Virginia where some of the other students had transferred because they had a great online program, but there was one big problem. It was expensive. I didn't have any student loans or anything like that, but it was like free school until you graduate, so it was a go. The idea of going to school at home was very appealing to me—I mean, hanging in pajamas and doing your homework or doing it out at the pool. I mean, what could possibly go wrong?

What could go wrong? Famous last words. If you have any tendency or inkling to be lazy, online schooling can be very difficult. And, of course, I had a very bad back, and not leaving the house meant that I become larger. The larger you become physically, the less you can do or want to do. I was maintaining at my new school, but I became a procrastinator and would just make a mad dash at the end of the semester to finish up all my work. Unfortunately, I got really good at doing this, and that became my *modus of operandi*.

I did eventually graduate with a bachelor's degree in religion. It only took me seven years. I started that journey in January 2000 and finished in August 2007. So much transpired during that time—the good, the bad, and the ugly, but the main thing is that God got me through it! Regrettably, I wasn't able to go to my graduation. I had wanted to walk across the stage so my kids could see their old man. Plus, I earned that piece of paper, you know. I had gone from not being able to properly put a sentence together to writing huge research papers to earning my degree.

I did go on to get my master's in biblical counseling. It was not the smoothest journey because during that time we had a lot of struggles with our daughter. And if you add the things that I already deal with it, it just wasn't a good time, but I made it through with the help of my professors. God truly orchestrated the right team at the right time. The two professors that I am referring to were also practicing psychologists, and they even gave me their personal numbers. They were just so amazing to me. The only sad part in this process was that I did not get to do my clinicals. I could not find one psychologist or psychiatrist, Christian or non-Christian, Martian, or anything who would throw me a bone. So, I did extra course work instead, oh yay! I didn't realize till like right now how badly it sucks that I didn't get those clinicals to become a licensed counselor. When I look for a new job, I see a lot of openings advertised for licensed counselors, and they pay really well. I'm qualified, but not qualified. I have the paper, though, ha-ha!

Aside from the craziness of school, all the heartache and pain, it leaves me wondering whether it all could have been avoided based on what I know now. But before those questions could be answered, we have to remember that they call me Job as my health took a turn for the worse.

CHAPTER 8

MY HEALTH TAKES A NOSE DIVE

It is amazing how many things can go wrong when weight gain spirals out of control. I honestly had no idea. I mean I knew about the biggies like diabetes and heart disease, but some cancers, gallstones, and a host of other issues can affect you. I was on the verge of a lot of these if I didn't do something drastic. I had tried every diet under the sun and would do well, but because I could not exercise or walk for any considerable amount of time, I would plateau in my weight loss. I wasn't sure what we were going to do. I was up to 426 pounds, and my ability to take care of the kids without help was sketchy at best. While Michele was at work, we wouldn't leave the apartment if at all possible. In 2003, Alana was eight and Greyson was six; they were great kids, but Greyson's nickname was Captain Destructo for a reason. It wasn't much of a life for the kids when they weren't in school, and I have to live with the realization that they were prisoners in their own homes growing up. I always tried to spoil them as much as possible because of the guilt I felt, and Lord knows that has come back to haunt us.

My parents had moved from Indiana to Florida with some of their friends, as a lot of people do when they retire. My dad also has a bad back and other joint problems, minus the weight problem. He kept saying that he had been feeling great since they moved to Florida. Michele and I were up for anything that could possibly help me feel better, and we knew that having help with the kids would be incredible. I knew my parents would also love to see the grandkids more, so the move was a no-brainer. We saved up enough money and moved to Florida in the winter of 2004.

Sunny Florida, here we come! We got down there, and sunny it was. We moved in to the same apartment complex as my parents, so the kids could see them all the time. It was a great complex for the kids and for me. The complex had wide-open spaces to run, a swimming pool, and a nice playground. It had a tennis court, weight room, and plenty of space to walk around the complex. With a great reference from the owner she had worked for previously, Michele had already secured a job with the chain salon as a manager. The kids got enrolled in school, and all was right in the world.

Summer 2005 was here, and it was our first Florida summer; the kids were so excited. We spent almost every day at the pool, in between the thunderstorms, that is. It was true, my back did feel better; I was more active, even playing tennis again. Not to the level that I had once played, but I was playing, nonetheless. I was getting more physical activity in a few short months than I had gotten in the past two years; maybe Ponce de León and I both had found our Fountain of Youth in Florida. Well, maybe not for longer life but for better quality of life anyway, and I was more than fine with that. Everyone was for that actually. We were doing things as a family again, but we shouldn't have started one family function again—that was eating out. At some point early after our move to Florida, I became a "secret eater." I would run errands on purpose just so I could get fast food, but I would still have to eat a regular meal at home so as not to arouse suspicion that I had gotten food out. There is no telling how many calories I was consuming in a day back then. If I had to guess, I would say 6,000 to 10,000 calories a day. It might have been more because every time I left the house, I would stop at a fast-food place; it was a sickness.

I had gotten so large that the staff at my primary doctor's office could not weigh me. That crap was embarrassing. I mean if I was like a professional sumo wrestler or something, that might have been something to brag about, but no, not this. Every time I went into the office and saw a new nurse, they would want to weigh me, and I would say that the scale doesn't go that high, and they would insist, because everyone always thinks that they know better. Isn't that the case, though, or is it just me? You know the answer to something, but no one listens. This has been my whole life. But I would oblige and get up on the scale and they would move the weight all the way over; then, they would move the other weight all the way over—followed by an awkward silence. For the first time in my life, my vitals were not looking good, which wasn't a shocker given all I was consuming. I was a borderline diabetic and a borderline this and that. So, the doctor prescribed fen-phen, and that didn't work. Then, he prescribed Prozac, and that worked for a while. I don't remember how much weight I lost, but it was minimal.

In August 2005, we found a group where I lost 70 pounds using the point system. See, because I am a very competitive person, it really helps me to be racing against others. In this group, I loved being the biggest loser every week, so it drove me. I loved the fact that I was wanted; I felt that I belonged. They call me Job, right? Nope, not this time. Florida was hit by three hurricanes, and all three of their eyes went over our town. It was like, "Welcome to Florida!" We didn't have electricity for what seemed like an eternity. The rain was coming in sideways; it actually came into our apartment and weakened one whole wall. You could literally push the whole wall back and forth with your hands. We had to cook on a BBQ grill in the breezeway of our apartment. We ate so much canned meat and other items that were not good for my diet. I mean these storms destroyed most of our area in Florida; there were blue roofs for years after these storms. When I say years, I can remember seeing blue roofs for over five years afterward. Now to explain what a blue roof is, it is a roof that has a blue tarp on it to cover a hole or a spot where the roof is leaking. These tarps were usually left in place because the homeowner hadn't settled with their insurance company.

This time was a mess for adults—no a/c, no electricity, but guess who loved it? The kids. They thought this was the greatest thing since sliced bread. They were already missing school and playing in the water, which in hindsight was very dumb on our part because in Florida, if you have water, you have to assume there may be a gator in it. But they played and played all day and just had a blast. Memories for them to last a lifetime, I hope anyway. I pray that Alana and Greyson never forget their best friends during that time, Ashley and Jacob. Side note, we used to babysit them a lot when their mom was going to school to become an RN, and now she is a nurse practitioner. So very proud of her!

After the storm, our apartment was no longer habitable. One wall was going to collapse at any time; water was throughout the apartment. We had three bedrooms, but no more three-bedroom units were available at the time. That was almost like a blessing in disguise because the rent was really expensive; however, it left us not knowing what we're going to do. Like always, my parents came to the rescue. But here is the kicker; they only had a two-bedroom apartment. So, we moved us four plus our two cats into their apartment. I think we had mattresses lined up against the wall in the living room or dining room where the kids would sleep at night; then we would put the mattresses back up in the morning, but we made it. We actually did that for quite a while.

In 2005, we bought a house together in a subdivision near the apartments where we had lived and across from the kids' school. So, it was easy for them to walk or ride their bikes to school. To get off my health for a moment, I should mention that it was in this subdivision that we met the family who introduced us to child acting and modeling. Since Alana was a baby, everyone had encouraged us to let her do some modeling. Well, this family told us how we would have control over what she would be doing, so we decided to give it a shot. For a child actor coming out of Florida, she did well. I would go with her even as big as I was; on one movie set, Shannyn Sossamon asked me if I was her bodyguard. We also got to spend a lot of time in Louisiana when she played the daughter of Tommy Lee Jones. She got to do a lot of awesome things and saw a lot, but looking back, I realize that the cost was too much. I will talk about that later.

My health was getting worse. I could no longer dress myself at times, bathe myself, or clean myself after going to the bathroom. This was a low point. If I had a gun at this time, I would have pulled that trigger till it fired. I'm crying now as I type these words because my wife had to do all these things for me. Take care of your back people, especially if you have never had a bad back; trust me, you don't want a bad back. On more than one occasion, I went into the bathroom to wash my hands and when I turned the faucet on or off, my back locked up with shooting, paralyzing pain, and I was laid up for days.

I was just washing my hands—not building a house, not changing a tire or something manly—washing my freaking hands! It didn't matter; the smallest thing could send me to bed for days. Also, eat healthy! I still have trouble with this and probably will until I die. It's probably because I wasn't made to eat certain things because I was the baby in the family, and my mom was just tired, and she would say, "Whatever." We get our kids to try everything. Even if they don't like it, that's cool, but at least they've tried it and found out. I still don't try different foods, and my kids ask, "Have you tried it?" and I say, "No, green stuff icky!"

Change was the key word for 2006. Change because my doctor told me I was going to die. By 2006, we did not even know how much I weighed, but he could look at me and my vitals and know that I was going to die if something drastic didn't happen. So, one day in his office he told Michele and me this; his statement was jarring, but we're not stupid, you know. He asked, "Have you thought about weight loss surgery?" He then said that it may be my only help because I could not exercise because of my back, and if I did not exercise, I would likely die. Even though I knew this, hearing it from a doctor was still tough. He gave us some pamphlets on some weight loss surgeries and clinics and then we went out to the car and cried.

The only thing I knew about weight loss surgery was that it would cost big bucks, and you could no longer eat large amounts of food. But because I was on Medicare and the surgery was medically needed, my doctor said that Medicare might pay for it. I mean, it was worth a shot. So, we called the clinic in Tampa and set up a consultation with a surgeon and his staff. We met with the doctor and he told me how the surgery worked and how much weight I would lose; it was so exciting! I was on cloud nine! I was like, "Sign me up!" I didn't even mind that I would have to do some counseling and lose some weight on my own first to show that I could handle the surgery post-op. I was just so excited by hearing about those pounds coming off like butter melting on a hot baked potato. Hey, I was still chunky, so I can still use that analogy. Then, we met with the surgeon's wife who was the scheduler and finance person. She had great news; I love great news: Medicare would pay for the hospital and the procedure, but it wouldn't cover the surgeon's fees, which were $10K or $16K—I honestly cannot remember. It could have been a million because ain't nobody got that lying around. She said if we financed his fees, he would not do the surgery till it was paid off, and looking at the options, I could be dead by that time. At this point, we knew I weighed over 525 pounds because the scale he had in his office went to 525, and I weighed more. So, we smiled like we always did and said, "Well, we have to pray about it," and we left. (That's also our go-to phrase to get salespeople off our backs; it works too!) But we went to our car, dejected; we just cried together. I knew I was going to die. I was going to be buried in that "bleeping" piano case is what I said to Michele. She had to drive us home. When we got home, the kids were happy as always, but I just went to our room. Michele told my parents the news. They didn't have that kind of money; no one did.

Once again, I was raising my white flag. What else could I do? But God wasn't done; He spoke to my parents in a big way. They came to us and said, "What if we refinance the home and use that cash to pay for the surgeon's fee?" I remember feeling like, whatever, I was tired of being let down, but Michele was always the optimist, and she asked, "Do you think it will work?" That is when they said, "It already has!" God used my parents to save my physical life! My parents have always done this, though, and they still do! So, I jumped on the phone, called the doctor, and said sign me up! My surgery was set for December 16, 2006, which is also my sister's birthday. I wish it could have been sooner, but I had to do that counseling to make sure my head was right, and I also had to prove that I could lose up to 50 pounds on my own before the surgery. I knew that would be a long six months, but I was so pumped for this new life. Then the unexpected happened. Remember? Our miracle baby, Keegan. This is when we find out that Michele was pregnant with him, and it was like, "YESSSSSSS!!!!" God was just showing off, you know!

December 16, 2006, arrived; I was nervous. I had never had surgery, so I was scared. Michele said that I was crying to her, telling her over and over how I loved her and saying what if I don't wake up and all of that. The person who had wanted to die his whole life was afraid of dying; go figure. The doctor came by and said that I would be okay and that they would come for me in a bit. He said, "Hang in there." I remember being in the operating room because of the sense of embarrassment; I was lying on a table, naked; they had to move me from one table to the next. They had trouble moving me, and

I was trying to help, and one of the guys was getting frustrated because I was so heavy. Knowing that I weighed 525 that morning at the hospital meant that, at my heaviest, I might have weighed anywhere from 550 to 600 pounds. Once I was on the operating table, they put a mask on and it was all over, because when I woke up I was in my room and feeling no pain.

Here is the crazy thing, from that day on I have never needed my CPAP machine; I didn't even snore! Michele was in heaven! I was no longer borderline anything, and the weight did melt off like butter, baby! I was losing it so fast that I was having to buy new clothes almost weekly. People didn't recognize me from week to week; it was hilarious. I could go into stores and walk past people or even talk to some, and they wouldn't realize who I was unless I was with Michele. I dropped from 525 to 260 pounds in a year. Maybe it was less than a year. Either way, Michele and the kids had a new man, new husband, and new father! The funniest thing is that Alana and Greyson do not even remember me being that big. It is wild how the mind works. But what I would give to go back and do those years over with them, to be the thin dad with them.

For the next six years, I rode four-wheelers, hiked through slot canyons, boated, and did everything under the sun that I couldn't do while I was a prisoner in my own body those many years. It was such a miserable existence when you are trapped inside your own body, and you want to do something but can't because your body doesn't work. But thankfully those years were behind me.

But they call me Job.... Come on, you knew it was coming, ha-ha! Christmas Day 2012, we went out as family. I cannot say much about what happened because I was a part of litigation in the matter and possibly signed something to keep me from talking about it. But, I fell, and it was just messed up. I hurt my back, got a bad concussion that lasted for a very long time. It was very frustrating to go from pain-free to having my back killing me again and restricting my day-to-day life again. The headaches were also unreal; I had never had migraines before this incident; afterward, I was diagnosed with migraines with aura and occipital neuralgia. The migraines with aura were absolutely horrible as they can mimic a stroke and landed me in the hospital twice. One time, when I was a schoolteacher, it happened while I was teaching! It was not a good experience. I'm just lucky the kids didn't pick my pockets. I was getting threats on a regular basis from middle schoolers. It was a tough school. I thought it was funny, but Michele did not think so. They had to take me away from the school that day by ambulance; that was my last day.

My back was getting so bad again that it was locking up the same as before; then, I would be laid up for a few days, then repeat. My doctor finally referred me to a specialist and let me tell you about my first impressions. I probably should have left and never returned, ha-ha. They forgot about me in the examination room; I waited for three hours before they realized their mistake. Yes, a normal person would have said something, but I'm not normal, as y'all should have seen by now. They did some X-rays and ordered physical therapy that he also offered in-house. The therapist was awesome. His name was Roman; he was from New York and just the coolest guy. I always loved going to therapy even though I knew it was going to hurt. I went through six weeks and nothing was improving, so the doctor ordered an MRI and started doing some injections. The MRI was inconclusive or unspectacular or whatever they called it. They saw thinning of my discs but nothing to do surgery on. That was good news because my dad had three back surgeries, and he was always worse after them. Everyone I had ever known was worse after back surgery, so I was relieved. So, let's load up on the therapy and injections.

My time with Roman was fun, but it wasn't helping. He could see I was in an insane amount of pain. I was crying to him at times. We had become friends; we were even officially Facebook friends and everything. I even heard him talking to my doctor's nurse practitioner and explaining that he had tried everything. That is when they talked to me about surgery, almost like it was going to be an exploratory surgery. So, they sat Michele and I down to let us know what was going to happen during the surgery and how routine it was. Let the circus begin! Circus? you say. Oh yes, we got to the hospital that morning and were told that the surgery would be four hours long, so remember that number. Then I got in my gown and was hooked up to an IV, the doctor decided that he wanted a new X-ray. So, I had to be taken to the X-ray department and then wheeled back into the surgery waiting area. Right before they started pumping in the feel-good stuff, the doctor's nurse practitioner came in and delivered some news. I swear this is 100 percent truth, and I have pictures to back this up, ha-ha. He said that the doctor did not like the hospital's X-rays and wondered if Michele could drive me back to his office and take some and then come back. I am not kidding! I am in my gown! But he is my surgeon, and what option do I have? So, they left the IV in but put a cap on it; I was still wearing my gown, but at least I got to put on shorts. We then drove over 20 miles to his office, took a couple of X-rays, and drove 20 miles back. The toll booth operators got a kick out of me, and no, the doctor did not pay for the tolls FYI, ha-ha.

The surgery started, and four hours went by, then five, then eight, and finally just under twelve hours. Twelve hours! The doctor told Michele that when he went in and opened my back, it looked like a land mine had gone off in there. He had to fuse discs L5 to S1 of my spine, so it was a major surgery, to say the least. When I woke up from the surgery, I felt like something was tearing in both my arms. Everyone thought I was crazy and ignored me. One nurse was so rude about it that she was taken off my care. She was my overnight nurse, and it was just bad; we will leave it at that. Eventually, I got out of the hospital, and my right arm started to feel better, but my left arm and shoulder never did. Come to find out when I was on the table for almost 12 hours, they never adjusted my arms during the surgery. But when I talked to my doctor about it, it was like an insult to him. My doctor is a spine doctor; it wasn't as if I was asking him to treat my shoulder or anything, and he said, "Well, I will give you an injection." I said okay because I wanted some help with the pain. I mean, every time I moved my left arm, it felt as if something was tearing. But like I said, the therapist seemed as if he was insulted for some reason. Normally, when we went into the treatment room, he would use some freeze spray to numb the area before I got an injection in my back. So, I was thinking he would do the same for my shoulder; nope, he just plopped that needle right in. I thought I was going to jump out of my skin. I guess I was right, he was a wee bit upset.

Well, I got to continue my back therapy with my friend Roman, and he would also work on my left arm and shoulder on the side. He couldn't get it unfrozen or whatever the problem was, and he said, "You need to go get it checked out." So, I went back to my primary for a referral to a shoulder specialist.

I got an injection with freeze spray, got therapy, but nothing worked. I was striking out on these injuries; then, I had surgery number two. The doctor stated that this one should be a piece of cake with two possible outcomes: (1) I would wake up and be able to start physical therapy pretty much right away, or (2) I would wake up and have to wear a sling for 30 days and then most likely need to have a manipulation done. I didn't even know what a manipulation was, but I was like, whatever.

So, I woke up and was told that I would have to wear a sling. Why? Because they had to shave off some bone, and that tearing I felt was my muscle. He had to screw the muscle to the bone. Now, for the manipulation after the month in the sling. My arm was frozen, and they had to go in and unfreeze it. That sounds harmless, right? I thought it did. Then, they said, "We have to knock you out because you do not want to be awake for this, not just for the pain, but also for the sounds that your shoulder is going to make." I was like, "Holy cow!" I was very glad to have been knocked out! I went to therapy after that, and I pretty much have full range of motion again.

Of course, I already told you about me dying, which was nuts, but that has been my life story. That was 2016, and as I write this, it is 2018, and all has been well until recently. Yep, say it with me: "They call me Job." I am here in Texas, doing the same job that I had in Florida, working as a CPS investigator. In the county near us, which is where Austin is located, they are short-staffed for CPS investigators. Well, they put out an email a couple of months ago asking for volunteers to help them out. I like to help people out, and I also like a change of pace, so it was a win-win for all of us. I signed up for almost a month because Greyson was going to be coming into town for a visit, and I would be on vacation after my time in Austin. So, when I came back from vacation, I would have a zero caseload, which would be awesome! That's every investigator's dream. I was on my last week, next to the last day before heading back home when I got into an accident. Get this, a one-car accident! They call me Job! Seriously, I was traveling down 71 East at highway speeds, and I was in between two cars and behind a nice Dodge Challenger. Well, the Challenger drove over a 4 x 4 sheet of plywood, and it shot out from underneath the car and into the air. It was first positioned as if I was going to drive through it! I thought I was going to die! Then at the last second, it dropped down and impaled the front of my car! I had plywood sticking through the grille of my car! I never would have believed it myself if I hadn't lived it.

Unfortunately, it wasn't only the car that took damage; I was diagnosed with whiplash, which caused benign paroxysmal positional vertigo and hurt my back. My stupid back again, ugh! Benign paroxysmal positional vertigo (BPVP) is something that I had never heard of, and I had never even had vertigo, so this was all new to me. Interestingly, BPVP is when the crystals in your ears get dislodged, making you dizzy and lightheaded. Well, mine was pretty extreme and took several therapy sessions to get figured out and corrected. I actually fell and cut my forehead open before they got it worked out. I ended up doing over two months of physical therapy because of this seemingly simple accident. I was thankful to our insurance adjuster for explaining to me the dynamics of the accident and the impact of even a 4 x 4 piece of plywood plus a vehicle moving at that speed to my body. I beat myself up for a long time after the accident because I had to be on workman's comp and only brought in 60 percent of my salary. It is hard enough to make it on one salary and then losing almost half your income even if it wasn't your fault was still hard to take. It was just a reminder of how life was back when my health was always an issue that caused us to be in a bind. I think I will always be hard on myself, despite knowing that God says I am good enough.

How do I know that I am good enough? Because I have worked in church most of my adult life, and that is what I would tell you, silly!

CHAPTER 9

MINISTRY AND I AIN'T SUGARCOATING BABY

B y far, this was one of the hardest chapters to write. There has been so much pain and suffering, but like my sister once told me, "Some of the greatest lessons learned are from the painful moments." Let's just say that I have learned a lot; heck, I have earned a PhD! But this chapter will be an open and honest look behind the scenes of the ministries that I have been a part of. Please understand that not all churches run this way, and I am sure not all church planters are like used car salesmen, ha-ha. In fact, I know that, because I know plenty. This chapter is also not an attempt to attack or blame anyone or anything. It is just me looking back and seeing whether my diagnoses affected how I handled certain situations and whether that is what caused things to go the way they did. This is why I won't speak of towns, church names, or give people's names.

To be fully transparent and lay all my cards on the table, I am going to disclose something that only Michele knows. Remember when I talked about how I had friends who were witches and Satan worshipers? And remember that when I went off to school, I didn't know anything about anything? Okay, don't laugh. You promise? Okay. I thought I was going to become a "Baptist Exorcist." I literally thought that was a thing, and I was going to do it. Then, I saw a TV documentary making fun of a guy saying sort of the same thing.

So, I guess only the Catholic Church has exorcists. Now, some of you might be wondering, "Why in the world would he think he would be an exorcist?" Let's just say that I have seen things through the years and experienced things, and I am in tune with things. Now, please, don't throw the book down and run out screaming, "Heretic!" For some reason, God has chosen me to have a heightened sense of discernment. That's what I call it anyway. Michele always brings me when she meets new people because I can read people—their motives and how they are as people. I can also tell when people are lying. The kids hate me because they cannot get anything over on me—or very little over on me. The weird thing is that on several occasions, people that I didn't know have told me that they saw dark objects around as if they were attacking me. Strangely enough, that is what I saw in my hospital room when I was coming out of my coma. I don't know what it all means; nor do I really care, as I cling to John 10:28: "I give them eternal life, and they shall never perish; no one will snatch them out of my hand." So, when I read and meditate on that, I have 100 percent confidence that Jesus has got me.

My time in ministry was not all bad; actually, most of it was amazing. I got to see God do some amazing things! On more than one occasion, I saw needs met for the exact dollar amount. Checks received for the exact dollar amount! That happened to us once; it almost gave me a heart attack; I was so blown away. God is so good! Most of my ministry positions were done on a volunteer basis, or as an "intern." From 1999 to 2008, I was receiving social security disability, so I could not take a salary because I could not afford to lose my Medicare. Since I had a pre-existing condition, I wouldn't be covered on anyone's insurance policy. So, the churches would give me stipends or pay me just under what I was allowed to make without losing my social security benefit. The churches didn't mind, as they were getting an almost free youth pastor, VBS director, AWANA Leader, and whatever else they needed. I didn't mind either because I wanted experience, and I wanted to serve and see lives changed. What I loved most about doing ministry work was the fact that it wasn't me. I could take no credit for any successes that I had over the years. That concept is so foreign to so many outside ministry but, in my case, it had extra special meaning. Outside the ministry world and in some aspects of the ministry world, it is all about me; look at what I did;

look at what I created; and of course, people stand back and take credit for it. I was always so uncomfortable, especially around adults, that I could not take credit for anything good that came from something I did. Before anything I did, I would get the worst case of the butterflies. I would spend enormous amounts of time in prayer and preparation before even the tiniest event or Sunday School class. I would humble myself and confess to God in prayer that I knew I was not qualified to even open His Word, but I also thanked Him for choosing me and asked Him to send the Holy Spirit to intercede on my behalf. He never let me down. He is always faithful. It's funny because I am not a fan of people, but I love people. I genuinely want to see people succeed and live the life that God has called them to live.

My first experience in official ministry was in Indiana before I went off to school and learned a little something. I would fill in for the pastor in the pulpit, but my main gig was teaching the senior adult Sunday school class. For both roles, my approach was to surrender in prayer and ask God what He wanted me to tell His people. The Sunday school class was a little easier because they had their curriculum already, and I would just go off that. Well, I thought it was going to be easier. The books they had were pretty shallow, so we used the books as a springboard for some really amazing discussions. I learned that a lot of the people in the class were going to that church not because that was their denomination, but it was where all their friends went. These discussions would end up going way off target, and I was not qualified for most of them. We would talk about how the Catholics, Methodists, Presbyterians, and Northern and Southern Baptists taught on various subjects. The great thing was that it made me work hard because I had to prepare for every possible question and rejection. It was hard, but it was so much fun. The people loved like it was going out of style, and they always brought goodies for me and my family to eat. It was so hard to say good-bye to them when we went off to school, but I always loved getting the cards of encouragement and care packages.

When we went off to school, we wanted to get plugged in to a church right away and volunteer to gain more experience. The church we found was a larger one of around 2,500 people, and they were always looking for students to come on board to help out. We had never been to a church that was this large; the band was incredible; the pastor wore jeans and his shirt was untucked. This was not what we were used to. It was like sensory overload for us, ha-ha. It was awesome, though, and they welcomed us right in. One of my professors was on staff, and he immediately put me to work in the youth department. I observed for a few weeks and got to know the other workers and a lot of the kids. It was cool! Their youth room was like nothing I had ever seen before; it was like a club that I used to go to back in the day—it was that well done. I was soon taking over some of the duties on Wednesday nights and one of the junior high Sunday school classes. But that was the extent of what any of the students could do. We could never teach on Wednesday nights to the larger groups even if we felt God had given us a Word. I was just a college freshman, so I wasn't voicing any concerns or issues with it. I actually didn't have one as I am typing with hindsight knowledge, and I didn't know there was a problem with it until other students started leaving to go to other churches. The youth pastor's dad was one of the deacons at the church; the pastor was also a student at the school I attended. Let's just say that there was a lot of politics going on before I got there and after I left. Another thing I learned about being at school was that new churches popped up almost daily! Seriously, it was like all the seminary students believed, "I can do church better" or "I have a new and improved way." This small town had so many churches that it was obscene. I bet the townspeople who didn't go to church thought we were all insane.

We were at one church for a year, and it was a great year! We saw Alana come to know the Lord and get baptized there, and that was amazing. But a group of our friends heard of a church, not a new church but a very old and historic one, that had recently called a seminary student as their pastor and had exciting things happening. Our next-door neighbor and good friends had gone to be a part of this excitement. Word had gotten back to the new pastor that I was doing good things, and he was interested in speaking with me about coming on as his new youth pastor. There were two major issues. They had a youth pastor in place, but he was supposedly on his way out already, and the other issue was that the new pastor jumped in and started making big changes. That is something else I am writing about in hindsight. But trust me, these two issues ultimately paled in comparison to what I am about to tell you.

First, let me tell you about this pastor; he was amazing, and he had a true heart for God's people and loved on everyone. His wife was the same way, and their children were the perfect image of little Noman Rockwell children. I'm actually rambling, but they were perfect. they didn't even run around the church, ha-ha. His sermons were on point and solid theologically. As I said, the church was a historical one and had some strong families that controlled the church from behind the scenes and were causing some issues. So, the pastor called in a speaker to address some things, but that didn't work. Then, one Sunday morning, the church was packed, and he was on fire; the sermon was great, then, he did something I had never seen. He went back to the chairs behind the pulpit and then came back out front and started preaching again. Then, he made some comments, "If you aren't going to do this or that" or "follow God's Word on this or that," then he started ripping pages out of what looked like his Bible. People were gasping! Literally gasping as he was doing this. It was a very powerful visual, and it hit home for a lot of people in the sanctuary, and to the others, it made them dislike him all the more. So, who knows what is happening in the hearts of people unless, as in this case, the pastor went on vacation two weeks later and on a Sunday night, he got voted out by a surprise vote. I remember sitting there and crying, heartbroken for this family. He wasn't even there to defend himself. By the way, he wasn't tearing up a Bible; it was a softbound journal. As I was leaving the church that night, I was contemplating whether I was going to stay in light of what had happened, and I simply said that there was no way that I could.

The next church we went to was at the invite of a professor, the one who named the "Lockian Theory." This church was interesting as it was our first look into a real deal "church plant." They had a senior pastor, two main financial backers, and a lot of deacons. There were no youth pastors or children ministry pastors. If a position was not mentioned in the Bible, then they didn't have it. Everyone stayed in the sanctuary together during the service and then afterward, they all ate together. They felt that they were the closest thing to, or striving to be the closest thing to, the example of the first-century church. It was interesting, but what it turned out to be was a homeschool group that had the same beliefs and then it grew into a church. But as someone who felt called to be a youth pastor, we did not become members because that church did not believe in having youth pastors.

I worked at one more church before we left for Florida due to my declining health. This church was an established church in the community, smaller building, but they had two services. The early service was a traditional one, and the second was a contemporary one. It was funny because both services were done by the same staff, but they would take off their ties and jackets for the contemporary service. I think that was technically the definition of a contemporary service, ha-ha. But the first service was filled with the people who were non-seminary students and a lot of families of all ages. The funniest thing was when the first service was over, the second crowd, which was all hip seminary families in blue jeans, shorts, T-shirts, and flip flops, would mix with the "Sunday's Best" crowd, but it worked. It was awesome! We would stand around and eat donuts and drink coffee together while they went to Sunday school, and we went into the service. It was a perfect example of how everyone can work together for the common good no matter their background.

I learned so much from the staff at that church. I was blessed to be their discipleship pastor for just over a year. I believe I did well in this position because it was a small group setting, and the people wanted to be there; heck, they signed up for it. I grew so much spiritually during this time. The staff meetings weren't just, "Let's pray and plan." They were deep; the pastor led us through a devotional time and would lay hands and pray for each and every one of us. Then, we would have real-talk time—sharing what we were struggling with on a personal level in our family or on a spiritual level. He genuinely cared and was a shepherd. One of the most amazing things that I learned was how this pastor did the Christmas services; he took the viewpoint of Mary, a historical viewpoint of a girl in that time and from that area. It was so moving, and I had never heard it done that way, and I have never seen it done that way again. I don't really understand why his approach is not used more often because it was a very powerful image of a 12- or 13-year-old girl being betrothed to a man who may have been around 30 years old. Maybe today's culture does not permit the story to be told from Mary's viewpoint, but that is how he did it. He showed her as strong and fearless, being completely reliant on God at all costs, even death, and she didn't waver. It was touching, moving, and beautifully done. We were all sad to go, but my health was failing, and moving to Florida was the right thing to do.

When we landed in Florida, I was no way ready to go into another ministry position. So, we just started attending the church that my parents went to. It was neat to see that some of the people from Indiana who had been in my senior adult Sunday school class were also attending there. My parents and some of their friends had relocated to the same area, and it made the transition easier for them all. Well, as you know, we had small children during this time, and this church had a lot of small kids that parents would just drop off or send to church while they either slept in or did errands or chores. A lot of these children didn't grow up in the church, and of course, they didn't know how to act in church. I know that sounds bad, but you know what I mean. They would run around, talk, and laugh loudly—just being disruptive is what I am saying.

This was the beginning of a very valuable lesson. Just because there is a need does not necessarily mean there is a call. But great things can still happen because it is God who is at work regardless of a call or not. The church had a youth pastor who was also the music minister. This guy basically ran the church through the family cliques who held the money. I know that sounds bad, but this is how it is in a lot of churches. Sad, but true. Of course, this information about the guy was not known at the time, but as this all played out, I wish I had known in advance, as you will see. Well, word got back that I had done some ministry work and was in school; the pastor was a nice guy, and he asked me if Michele and I would do something with the children's church. I had never done children's church, but how hard can it be? Ha-ha, famous last words. I found out how many youth want to help out if it gets them out of "big church." Shocker, right? So, we figured out quickly that we needed to keep them busy! Music, crafts, and then I would do a mini-sermon. It was a winning combination. Kids were starting to bring their friends, and it was awesome. I felt convicted that I should also be explaining the gospel to them and giving them an opportunity to respond. Respond they did, but what I would do was also allow them to respond in "big church" as well; that way they could explain to the pastor about the decision they had made.

I mean he was the one who would be officially talking with their parents and baptizing them if that was their choice.

God was doing great things, and people were noticing. However, it wasn't all positive attention. The youth were flocking to the new children's department; the department started with six or seven kids and grew to more than 20 kids. Not a lot of parents coming, but there were plans in the works to address that. Summer was upon us, and that meant VBS! But they did VBS their way and had their lady who was the director and so on. Well, I was a bull in a china shop. I was like, well, I am officially the children's pastor, so I should just take VBS on, and so I took it on. I just took the bull by the horn and made some people upset. That was another lesson learned in ministry. (When you are new to a church, never make major changes right away unless they are desperately needed.) But because of how I am with all my many diagnoses, I looked at VBS and asked: How can we streamline this? How can we make this easier and foolproof? I made it so that the director didn't need to be bothered the whole week unless there was a problem. I also introduced prizes and giveaways to increase attendance. Apparently, this was revolutionary in 2004 because a lot of their heads were going to explode. The results were great; they usually averaged in the 30s, and we averaged in the 70s. But the best part that none of us could take credit for was that we had 32 kids accept Christ that week. It was like, "Bam! God was just showing off!" Of course, after this and the end of summer, we had three hurricanes hit our area in Florida.

The next event would have been Halloween, but the church did not do an event or a Harvest Festival; they do such events now I believe, but back then, they were completely frowned upon. Then came Thanksgiving. The children's department had planned a big dinner—but, and isn't there always a but? We had plans on the calendar before the youth group did, but they complained loudly, and we had to move our event. There were only six people in the youth group. I was mad. I'm being real here with you. What made it worse or better for me was their event was a flop, and ours was a success. Yes, I am a horrible person. Christmas was next up, and they graciously said we could have it because I think they thought we would have the same fate as their event. But I had a secret plan. New youth and children pastors out there: listen to me clearly here. Senior adults are just waiting and willing to be utilized in any way possible. I also use them to start mentorship programs. They are an untapped gold mine in almost every church. Plus, they are excellent cooks and bakers. We taught the kids songs, so it wasn't just food; it was also an evening of entertainment. We had deep-fried turkeys and all the fixings with desserts galore. Parents came for this, and then they started coming on a regular basis, so it was a win-win.

Things didn't stay so good as I alluded to earlier. The youth group was basically nothing, and they wouldn't even do anything over the summer except for youth camp. The reason for this was the youth/music minister was also a schoolteacher, and he took the summers off because he felt that this was his time. So, these youth would basically do nothing, and everyone would wonder why the youth were not growing in numbers or spiritually. So, I offered to do things with them, and the youth started growing. Turns out that 1 + 1 = 2; it wasn't rocket science, and then it got to the point that everyone could not ignore it. The pastor talked with the youth/music minister, and he decided that he would just focus on music. He said he gave me his blessing, but when I made even the smallest change in the youth room or anything, it was met with resistance. It was extremely frustrating; he had youth who were loyal to him and would run and tell him everything. I went to the pastor and asked for guidance because I had honestly never experienced anything like this. He would always say, "Onward and upward." So, I just pushed forward.

The next few months were good; the youth and children's departments were growing. We had gotten other adults to start working with the kids on Sunday mornings, so we could get some "big church" time. Things seemed good, maybe too good. Then, one Sunday after church a guy came up to me and asked if I could meet him at someone's house around 3:00 p.m. that day. Now, I call him "a guy" because I can't remember his name, ha-ha. But he and the people where we were to meet were friends of the music minister, so I was baffled by the request, but I obliged because I was nice with everyone. These people were also very wealthy. When I got to their house, they offered me snacks and a soda; the house was beautiful. I had never been in such a nice house. They started talking to me almost like this was a job interview of sorts and then they started asking me questions about the pastor. Did I like him? Did he keep regular hours? What were staff meetings like? They asked a whole bunch of things. It was very awkward, and I told them my loyalty was with the pastor until he did something that was unbecoming to his position of pastor. If the pastor wasn't heretical or doing something that went against what the Bible says about the call and position of the pastor, I'm good. So, then, I was on their bad list. Their kids stopped coming to children's church and youth functions; it was ridiculous and sad for the kids because they were the ones losing out.

I didn't go home after that meeting; I went to a nearby park and talked out loud to God. Just asking him if this was what ministry was really like. Because this was shaping up to be another bad experience like when we were up north, and I didn't want anything to do with it. I didn't want anything to do with a church that does this to their own. I was too much of a babe in Christ for this. I couldn't handle it, honestly.

On Tuesday mornings, we would meet and pray and talk about life. It was like a miniature staff meeting for the pastor and me. We would meet on Tuesdays because the church office was closed on Mondays. So, at the end, I told him everything, and he didn't seem surprised. He just sat there and was like, whatever. Man, I was like Peter; I was ready to grab my sword and go to town! He was reserved and way more mature than I was in my faith, clearly. I didn't know it, but this was his first position as a senior pastor. Maybe he didn't know what to do or how to fight back or what. Time went on, and things spread through the church like the plague. Soon the church was split with one group sitting on one side and the other group sitting on the other side. I wish I was kidding. But he took it, never said an ill word and then one morning at the end of the service, he brought his wife and two children on the stage and announced that they would be leaving. He stated that he would rather leave than cause the church to split. I wept like a baby at what I saw; the selflessness and humility he showed that day still sticks with me like it was yesterday. I remember seeing his whole family displaying so much grace as they hugged the very people who pushed them out. The tears rolled down their cheeks, but they showed Jesus; they showed the beauty of the true meaning of the gospel that morning in that sanctuary. I remember going in to shake his hand because I didn't show emotions, as that is not me, and he grabbed me, and we hugged and wept together. No words were necessary. I was like, where is my sword, ha-ha! I never stepped foot in that church again. But God was working that morning in the hearts of those people. I think it was the fact that there he was, with his family, displaying such humility and grace. That may have been like Peter's sword to their heart! That pastor and his family and I are still friends to this day. A few years ago, we actually had a few good laughs about all this and how that every single one of the major players except the music minister came to him and asked for forgiveness.

We almost worked together at another church; it was at his next stop actually. I was helping their youth department over the summer. I was like, what madness is this? Anyway, things were going well and the people who were doing it stepped down, and that created a spot. The couple who led the youth program did it for free as they were independently wealthy, so money was not an issue for them. This church was known as kind of tight for being a larger church. If you are in youth ministry, you will understand this. If a church can get away with getting a full-time youth pastor for free, they will do it every time. Now, there are some great churches that won't take advantage of students, but a lot of them will throw that intern tag on you. It usually didn't bother me to have the intern tag or whatever, but if I was going to be the full-time guy, then I wanted them to call me to be the youth pastor. Don't tell me you feel guilty about not calling me because you cannot afford to pay even if I agree to a stipend. Just be honest with me. I love honesty, don't you? I am also not a big fan of pastors who know which people are tithing and have discussions with people about it. I feel that the less the pastor has his hands in the money, the better. That is all I will say about that.

(*Tip #1012:* When you are interviewing for a position, never criticize anything because the person doing the interview might have been the one who came up with that idea.)

In 2007, my weight was coming off fast, as I had had the gastric bypass in December 2006. I was feeling great; my back was doing much better with the extra weight off of it. So, Michele and I said, "Let's start praying about God opening that first paid position somewhere." I was feeling great enough and confident enough to get off disability. Oh, how amazing and freeing that would be. I was in the top three candidates for several churches, but it was always sad to get the inevitable rejection email, but life goes on. Then, I started corresponding with a pastor in Arizona, and we seemed to hit it off from the get-go. It was so good that I feared I was setting myself up for heartbreak. Then, all communication stopped—nothing. Come to find out the pastor had a heart attack and was in the hospital. Well, in a few weeks I got an email from the church secretary, asking me to fly out to meet the pastor who was recovering in a Phoenix-area hospital. I freaked out! I had never flown! I was always too big to fly, and my fears of falling kept me from even trying. The meeting went great, and then I went back home to wait. After a couple of weeks, I got another call, requesting Michele's and Keegan's information so we all could fly out to visit the city and the church and to teach a lesson to the high school and middle school youth groups. Oh, Keegan was coming because he was a baby; Alana and Greyson stayed home with my parents.

When we stepped off the plane, a group of youth and parents had signs and gift baskets waiting for us! It was so amazing, as no one had ever done anything like this for us before. It was just like a movie! We were already in love with these people! Still love those people! They had the week planned for us: sightseeing, eating amazing foods, and sitting down with the search committee. I had learned that they had just lost a very well-loved youth pastor and his family. In fact, they had three youth pastors in four years. But of course, they didn't put that in the job posting. I guess it's like being on a first date and they keep talking about how awesome their ex was; well, that was how this week was for me. The pastor was a cool guy, and he truly loved those kids, our kids. But I was so happy to be there, and I knew I was supposed to be there. I didn't even care to ask why the previous youth pastor was no longer there because it didn't matter. The visit went great, and when we left, it felt as if we were leaving family. We made it home, and it wasn't too long after that trip that we were called to be their next youth pastor.

When you start a new position, they call it the "honeymoon" period. Mine lasted longer than most, as I had the run of the place except on Sundays before I saw an elder. It was six months before I even saw the pastor as he was out still recovering. I'm not going to say much about this man as he has passed away, but when he did come back to work, he was not the same man that I met in Phoenix. Whether it was his medications or whatever, he just wasn't the same. Things immediately changed for the worse; I was suddenly in hell, and I was confused, sad, hurt, and about a million other feelings. I went to one of the elders about what I was feeling, and he opened up and said, "This is why you are the fourth youth guy in five years and why the church has lost members steadily ever since he became pastor." This was really hard to hear, as we had moved our family across country, and we were at a place where they go through youth pastors like it's nothing. When I took over, they ran about eight youths on average because the they were tired of losing people they loved. I don't blame them; at their age it is very hard to become attached to people and then have them ripped from you. So, every time, they lost a youth pastor, they would lose on average half the youth to a different church or to no church at all. But Michele and I poured ourselves into those kids, the workers, and their families. They came back, and we grew. We would have lock-ins with over a hundred kids, and for this town, that was really good. God was doing amazing things.

One of the greatest things that we started was a mentorship program with some of the senior adults and with the youth leaders, of course. They would match up with youth and meet with them once a week. Some would take them to lunch or, for me, I took mine to the golf course and spent some quality time with them. I mentored several students, including some future youth leaders, and they were always over at the house. (*Tip #1:* Set boundaries and keep them. Your home is for your family.) But I always had the mindset that 24 hours wasn't enough in a day and bringing the kids home with me was just more time I could spend with them.

Tragedy strikes . . .

One night, Michele and I were just finishing up at Walmart; we got in the car, and my phone rang. It is one of my youth's mom and a friend, and she said that she had something that she needed to tell me. So, Michele and I were sitting in the car, wondering what it could be. She told me that something might have happened to Alana with one of the senior high youth. I asked her how she heard this, and she said that she had intercepted some texts between her son and Alana. She said that I needed to call Alana right away, as she was expecting my call and that others were there with her. I was freaking out, but of course, I called, and one of my youth workers handed her the phone, and she was crying. Alana was crying uncontrollably, and she said something that no father ever wants to hear. She said, "He did me; I said no, but he did me." I told her it was going to be okay and that Michele and I would make sure that she was going to be okay and that we loved her. I said, "We will see you in a bit." I hung up the phone and started punching the roof of our SUV as hard as I could and saying, "I'm going to kill him!" Michele was trying to calm me down, but there was no calming me down. The guy in question was one of my senior high youth—one that I was mentoring. He was over at my home all the time! I had let this monster into my home! Well, his home was right down the road from the Walmart, and I tore off for his house like a bat—like you know what! I went there to kill him, no doubt in my mind that I would have done it too. But God had other plans, as no one was home. Right around the corner from his house was the police station, and we went there and informed them of what happened.

We immediately put Alana into counseling as we knew that the sooner the healing process began, the better for her. The one thing that we never thought about was the toll it would take on all us as a family, individually and professionally. All loss needs to be grieved because if not, it will manifest again; trust me. We had to deal with some issues, such as this town was small, very isolated, and the rumors were already flying as this guy was arrested and released. His family was very prominent and very well liked. I was getting hate emails and calls about how could I dare ruin this young man's life. One of my favorite ones was how could I, as a pastor, seek to get justice against a young man, and how two tragedies will help no one, so I should let this go. I put on a brave face and I would say the right things, but inside God knew the truth; I was filled with a burning hatred for Him. I mean, He allowed my 12-year-old daughter to be raped; He didn't deserve my love and devotion. He didn't deserve crap! I mean, we moved all the way across the country and for what? Pain and misery? Are you kidding me right now, God? I knew a couple of things. First, my daughter could not stay in that town while that guy was out running around getting drunk and high and spreading whatever he wanted while we said nothing, so we began to think about heading back to Florida.

I was also facing another issue, a showdown with the pastor; the work environment had become so toxic that I no longer went anywhere near him after some comments he had made. People were coming to me and saying, "Please wait this out." They said that they were going to do something about him, but what they didn't know was there was no way we could stay in that town for our daughter's sake. So, an elders' meeting was called to see if our relationship was too far gone to be reconciled, and so they laid out a plan and I refused to budge, but to my surprise, he refused as well. We both dug our feet in, and with the counsel from the association, they let both of us go. Here is the kicker, I refused to work with him because I had already decided we were going back to Florida, and I was doing the church a favor by getting him to leave as well. Isn't the mind a sick thing? How we can justify things?

But I wasn't in my right mind; I was in full grief mode with a huge helping of bitterness, so I really thought I was doing the right thing. I mean the numbers really did take a nosedive, and people had come to me wanting him gone, so it didn't take much to make that leap. So, there I was standing before the kids, the helpers, and parents saying good-bye, feeling like I had accomplished something. What an idiot I was. A lot of those youth never went back, still aren't in church because of what I did. I will have to answer for that. I also reached out to that pastor before he died, asked for forgiveness, but he never responded. I like to think he never got the email, that it went to his junk email folder. (The young man got six months in jail and 10 years' probation in which he had to register as a sexual offender.)

We went back to Florida and as far as I was concerned, I was done with ministry work. When we got back, I worked in insurance, but that only lasted for 10 months. Things were starting to affect me more than I thought; I was showing signs of anxiety, which was at times paralyzing while I was at work. So much so that one weekend I had four doctors tell me that I needed to quit. Still running from God, I was refusing to go to church, but the kids would go with the grandparents. Something was happening with Alana that we were unaware of as well. See, she is my adopted daughter, and for her whole young life, we had been struggling with how and when to tell her because her biological father was a bad guy, a really bad guy. Well, while we were in Arizona, we told her, and she took it well. She didn't even blink, or so we thought. What we didn't know was that a senior high youth girl had befriended her; this girl had a horrible home life and was jealous of the life that Alana had. (She admitted this to us a few years ago after she heard what Alana had been up to.) This so-called friend of hers was actually telling her that because I wasn't her "real" dad, she didn't have to listen to me anymore. See, we thought this new behavior that Alana was exhibiting was due to what had happened to her, so we continued the counseling in Florida. Then, I got a call from one of the neighbors saying that their daughter told them that Alana had a burn on her arm and that Alana had told her daughter that I had burned her intentionally. Thankfully, we were great friends with them, and they called us first before they called CPS on me. We had the neighbor and their daughter come over; then we had Alana come sit down in the living room and she was probably freaking out because she looked so nervous. With everyone there, we asked Alana how she burned her arm. She had to admit that she burned it baking cookies. I wish this was the only stunt she pulled, but they would get worse.

From insurance to teaching school. For the 2010–2011 academic year, I taught at Mulberry High School, in Mulberry, Florida. I taught regular and honors world history and government and economics. It was so rewarding to see history come alive and help the students realize that if we don't learn from the mistakes of the past, we are bound to repeat them. In many ways, teaching is like being in ministry. I was trying to justify not doing what I was called to do. I loved teaching, so I felt like I was reaching tons of kids. I haven't said it in a while—but they call me Job. The district thought they would be 20 million dollars in the hole, but they ended up being 60 million dollars in the hole. How does that even happen? But they did it, and all first-year teachers were let go. That was in 2011. I was informed in April, so at least I had plenty of time to find a new job.

By this time, we had started going to church as a family again, and we started to receive counseling for Michele and me for all that we had gone through with Alana in Arizona, what Alana was doing now, and how all this had been affecting us as a couple. Alana proudly admitted that she was trying to cause us to divorce because, in her mind, Michele would for some reason find her ex from almost 17 years before and make a love connection. Well, we weren't breaking up, and even if we did, Michele would never go back to him of all people. Anyway, the pastor of the church plant we were attending was a friend of mine, as we were associated a few years back. He was also pretty well known in church planting circles, so it was kind of a cool thing when he asked me to join his team. He was well briefed on why I left the church, my anger toward God, and he was the one who hooked us up with this really great counselor. He still felt that God wanted me on the team. So, we prayed about it and sought a lot of wise counsel about it. A lot of people said that I should not do it, including a lot of my family because it didn't make sense because this new church plant could only pay $750.00 a month. But it was like I said, with God, it has never been about the money and it will never be for us; it's about seeing lives changed.

Okay, I think people see my size and go, "Oh, crap!" and then when they get to know me and realize that because of my diagnoses and how that makes me wired, it makes me an easy target, and they just walk all over me. I wish this wasn't the case, not for my sake but for Michele and my family's sake because they get hurt the most by this. I was being recruited to become his next youth pastor because the one he had, quite frankly, was not very good, but he had skills and other talents that were very useful in the church planting world. See, sadly, in a lot of church plants, when they interview you, it's not about your calling; it's questions like this: "What do you bring to the show?" "How much equipment do you have?" "What software can you run?" "Can you make websites?" "Can you raise your own support?" It's a business, and they start them and then they leave them, but before they do, they have you sign some agreement in which they have to pay you a percentage for some time. I didn't have any of these skills, but I was called to be a youth pastor, and that's what I brought to the table. So, they were waiting to announce my "official position" title when they gave the old guy the axe. But then the pastor got word that someone he knew was thinking of moving from North Carolina back to Florida. Now, that guy was good at websites and was an okay youth pastor; his wife did most of the work. He was a great guy, but that is not the point. So, without saying anything to me, he demoted the guy on staff and somehow got him to stay on, because he had this huge trailer that held all our church stuff in it, and he was also our sound guy on Sunday mornings. But

I digress, ha-ha. We had a meeting and the pastor brought in the new guy who only one person had met, and he announced that he would be the new youth pastor. Maybe he could sense my dismay and shock; he pulled me aside and said to me, "Hey, I forgot to tell you that I wanted to give you a bigger role within the church and make you the family pastor, and you will oversee the children and youth ministry." I was like, okay, anything for the team. I went home and told Michele, and she was pissed because she knew exactly what had happened. We were back doing children's church, ha-ha! Nothing wrong with that, but I got played big-time, but hey it's all good because it was not about Michele and Jon.

We spent a couple of years there, and I started to notice a lot of things that were getting harder and harder to swallow. Like I mentioned at the beginning of the chapter, I had the ability to read people, and he knew this. One day, he asked me, "Can you read me?" This was after one of the guys had asked me to go with them to meet someone. I looked at him and said, "You know what, you are one person I can't read." He then said, "Wow, that's what people normally say about _____ (our music minister/main financial backer)." Things were never the same between us again. We both were gone shortly after that conversation. He went on to another promotion with some association, and I went on to start my own church as some had asked me too.

Now, I had been approached to start a church because they liked my style and how I taught. I had never felt the call to be a senior pastor, as I always planned on retiring as a youth pastor. This was early in 2012. Michele and I went through church planting classes through the convention, got sponsored, and away we went. Man, we made a lot of mistakes, like starting too big too fast, just expecting God to open the floodgates, and people would just show up at the house. We didn't have the financial backing like at the other church plant; ours and others like it started in homes much like the ones the disciples were meeting in after the ascension of Jesus. Little music, message, and then break bread together. It was awesome, though, and it felt right; families were coming, and we were growing. But they call me Job! I had that fall if you remember, the one we can't really talk about. Well, this made me less than reliable where the ole back was concerned. Some weeks, we were good to go with service; then others, there was little to no notice for everyone that my back was out. Needless to say, the church plant died, and more of me died with it. We dissolved basically into another church plant; we gave a lot of our stuff away to another church plant that was in need.

While at this church, things turned for the worse with Alana. She was 17, going on 35, and we found out that she was dating a scumbag of a 22-year-old without us knowing it. I can call him that as I knew him personally, and I am being nice. Come to find out she had been sneaking out and doing drugs, alcohol, and everything else with this guy. We didn't find out about this until Michele found the iPod that the pastor's daughter had given to Alana because she was grounded from electronics. Well, on her iPod, we found conversations between not just them but many different people. But the worst was that she was saying to him that she feared that I was going to rape her and him replying that he would never let that happen. I had friends who were local sheriff's deputies, and they said that it sounded as if she was trying to get him to take things into his own hands to protect her from me. It was after the fact, but immediately Michele woke Alana up, and we all were like, "What the heck is this?" She didn't deny it again, and it was right then that I no longer felt safe living in my own home.

In my eyes, Alana had won; I was going to leave. Then, Michele and I talked more later that night that her behavior wasn't going to change after Alana was yelling and proclaiming her love for her Romeo from the tops of her lungs. So along with Michele's dad and my parents, we all talked about Alana leaving the house. For one, I didn't feel safe after what we had read and if Alana stayed, she would most likely run away with this guy because she just said she would. So, we all talked, and then we called Michele's sister in Washington State, and she agreed to take Alana, and she was on a plane the next morning, so she wouldn't have a chance to run away. Well, once Alana got to Washington, she called everyone and had her own version of what happened. Michele and I never defended ourselves; we remained silent. So, that Sunday, I went to church; Michele didn't feel like going because this all happened on Thursday, and it was all too fresh. But I needed to be in church. At the end of each message, the pastor would always sit on a bar stool and just talk about his reflections or whatever was on his mind. Now, keep in mind this was a small church plant, maybe 50 people at the time on a good

Sunday. At the end, he sat there and looked at me, and please get this: he is my friend, my close friend, and he says, "I could never just throw one of my kids away." Are you freaking kidding me right now? If my back wasn't so bad, I probably would have body slammed him just then. But I was cool; I walked out, and three weeks later, I had surgery on my back. He came to see me in the hospital, and I did the biblical thing. I confronted him about his comments, especially when he was going off what a 17-year-old said.

That was the last ministry position I held. Is God through with me? I don't know. That's not for me to say. I mean there were a lot more churches I've worked at over my 15 years in ministry, and they weren't all bad. Actually, most of them were incredible experiences. Michele and I saw God move mountains many times, and if He chooses to call me back, I will gladly pick up the phone.

One of my favorite shows was on VH1, and it was about bands and where they are now, and I think I have one more chapter in me. So, in honor of that, I will give you a look at where we are now.

CHAPTER 10

WHERE WE ARE NOW . . .

Where are we now? That is a great question; but unfortunately, it can't be easily answered. You know they call me Job, right? Well, if you don't believe it yet, I'm sure this story might put you over the edge. So, I told y'all about the 4 x 4 sheet of plywood through the grille of my car. Well, that happened almost exactly a month before I wrote this chapter. So, I'm still going to physical therapy for the injuries.

Well, I was driving the other day, which was the one-month anniversary of the accident and about two weeks after I got my car back from the auto body shop. I was driving down I-35 South toward Austin; the speed limit is 75 mph, but traffic was doing 80 to 85. Next thing I know, a black object hits the front of my car! I freak out again, slam on the brakes, and almost cause a huge accident. But I didn't stop because I figured whatever it was it went under the car and was long gone. Next thing I know, a driver in a pickup truck was waving me down. I'm thinking, did I cut this guy off and he was road raging and we're going to fight right here or something, ha-ha. So, we pull over; I get out, and he runs up to the car and pulls this huge mud flap out of the grille of my car! In the exact spot where the plywood hit! Are you kidding me? He says to me, "Hey, I saw the truck it came from; if we hurry, we can catch up to him!" So, we were doing like 90+ mph to catch the truck driver. We finally caught him and got him to pull over. For a week, I have not been able to drive my car because the A/C blows hot air, and it's still in the 100s here in central

Texas—ain't nobody got time for that. The truck driver's insurance company finally got back to me and sent me to the same auto body shop that just did the previous work on my car. I'm sure they will get a good laugh out of this one. I mean what are the odds of one person in the same car getting hit in the same spot one month apart in the same way? It's just my life, ha-ha.

I said earlier that I have this weird, strange ability for perceiving things, not necessarily the paranormal but some pretty strange things, nonetheless. For a while, I had been having recurring dreams that my cancer was going to come back or that I would get some other form of cancer and ultimately die. The dreams were very real and would become more detailed the more I had them. This was going on for months and I never mentioned it to Michele because why bother her about silly dreams. Then, I started to notice that I was tired all the time even after a good night's sleep. Not only was I tired, but my focus and my desire to do anything were gone. I just wanted to stay in bed; my job, which was once my refuge, was getting to be a chore. This was embarrassing because I had a new supervisor, and I have always prided myself in how I handle myself at work and get my work done. Now, here I was not even wanting to be there, and in my line of work, that is not a good attitude to say the least. I had an appointment coming up with my endocrinologist, so I decided to wait to discuss this with my doctor. I went for my blood work and a week later, I went for the doctor's appointment. Appointments with my new doctor are always annoying because it's my fault that my previous doctor didn't send the right records, ha-ha. Every time for 10 minutes, he chews me out about this. As I sat in the exam room, I was already highly annoyed because quite frankly I don't do well when people treat me this way. Anyway, he started reading my blood work results. He went down the line of stats, making noises with each new line, and he asked me, "Are you taking the medications as prescribed?" I'm like, "Yes, sir, never miss a day." Then he says, "We have a problem then." The last time I saw him was a few months ago; I had an ultrasound, and it was all clear. The doctor said, "I'm going to send you to a specialist because they can do a different ultrasound and by looking at your blood work, I would feel better having someone else take a look." He said that my blood work had a tumor marker on it, and my levels were not where they should be. It was no big deal, and I walked out, as I would be notified when my appointment with the specialist would be. I texted Michele, "Not good news." She responded with, "It will be okay; we've done it before, and we will do it again! Love you!" I think at that point, I was numb; you know, I don't do well with emotion anyway, so it's like whatever. I mean, it was almost like my dreams had been preparing me for the unavoidable, so in a way, I almost welcome death. I mean hell, for my whole life, I have battled depression and suicide ideations, and heck, this could be my ticket home. I don't have to do a thing to get it punched. Yeah, that's what is weird about me and people like me; I have morbid and disturbing thoughts routinely, but people would never, ever know it.

In my job, I experience the same thing. I see dead children or badly abused or neglected children, and it doesn't faze me. I mean it bothers me that there is evil in the world, but so many people are like, "Wow I couldn't do your job!" or "How do you do your job?" I don't know; death or things like that have never bothered me. When I was younger, I had to teach myself how to react when people were hurting; I've noticed that Keegan and Greyson both struggle with the same thing. I promise I am not a cold heartless person; I just have some issues, I guess ha-ha.

Finally, the call came for me to go to the specialist. I don't remember why Michele wasn't able to go with me for this appointment, but it was a solo trip back to Temple for the doctor's appointment. I got there, and the nurse was flirting with me, ha-ha. She is around 60 years old and telling me I looked too young to have been born in 1971, so that was making me feel good. So, the mood was light; this is a teaching hospital, so my specialist had a fellow and a student from Texas A&M in the room, and they asked if that was okay and I said, "Sure." The doctor was a very nice lady, very upbeat and positive. She said, "We're going to do this ultrasound and then get you out of here as I don't expect to see anything since you recently had one done." So, I felt more at ease because of her confidence. She started the ultrasound on the left side of my neck as she was talking to the students and teaching; she said, "One side done." She moved to the right side, and as she moved the wand around, I heard, "Hmm, that shouldn't be there." Then, they all started talking to one another. Then, they wrapped it up and said they needed to do an emergency biopsy on whatever it was they saw. What they saw was a 2 cm spot on a lymph node that was sitting on my jugular vein. The doctor was trying to sugarcoat this, trying not to freak me out, and I said to her, "It's cancer." She was stunned and said, "Let's not jump to conclusions." I said, "Trust me, I know, and it's cool; I've known for some time." She was completely baffled, and then I explained to them about how they call me Job and how even my phone autocorrects my name to Job. I also let her in on how for the past few months, I had been having these dreams, but I left the dying part out. I didn't want her not to be my doctor, ha-ha.

They took me down to a procedure room. There was a lab technician in the room because once they did the biopsy, I would know almost immediately if it was, in fact, cancer. Cool that I wouldn't have to wait. So, the fellow sprayed my neck with some of that freeze stuff and injected some pain killer into the area because they said the procedure would be tough because they had to go through muscle. It was an interesting feeling because I wasn't completely numb, but I wanted to hurry up, so I endured quietly. They got four slides worth out of my neck, and the doctors left the room while the technician went to work. Once she was done, she went and got her boss who came in and looked through the microscope, wrote some notes, and walked out. The doctors came back in, and they had a sad look on their faces, and I said to them, "It's okay; I'm going to be okay." The doctor said that she was sorry and said that I was in good hands. So, they walked me down to a scheduler to get everything worked out. As I am typing this, the surgery is scheduled for this coming Friday. Hey, they call me Job!

Surgery was done, and I survived! They were able to get the lymph nodes out, all 53 of them. It wasn't just one with the cancer cells in it; they do not really know if this is the end of the surgeries. Yeah, it was hard to hear, but we know that God has this under control. Again, I am not scared to die, but if I do die, I will die proclaiming His name. It is vitally important for my kids and others to see that I live and die by what I say I believe. I think it is more important in the face of death to show this strong testimony than in life.

It's a Family Affair

What we have been going through has been a family affair, and it has also been affecting my mom in a hard way. She had to grieve that my brother and

I didn't get the help or all the help that Keegan has at his disposal. It's like I told my mom, there was nothing that she could have done; back in those days, they (some educators and a few parents) just labeled us as bad kids. Now, this does not apply to all teachers! So, calm down, ha-ha. But back in those days, there wasn't a lot known about different diagnoses. My brother was so off the chain that my mom was at the school every day! A teacher once told him to glue himself to his seat and, you guessed it, he literally glued himself to his seat! My dad is like a mathematical genius but can barely read; he dropped out of school in the eighth grade. He has a lot of sensory issues as well; he cannot be in crowds and always has to be moving and does not like loud noises. My brother is a genius but does not want any labels attached to him, and I understand. As I said before and I am sure will again, labels can affect how people see you, how employers see you. That can have far-reaching repercussions. Just for the record, my brother has no official diagnoses. Are you happy now, Don? Ha-ha!

Now, an update on where we are with our immediate family, namely Keegan. It is complicated because it is different from day to day with Keegan. Sometimes, even moment to moment can be challenging. But the more we learn and the more we grow, the better Keegan does. Keegan and kids like him need to feel the reassurance of the love of everyone around them. They need to feel as if they belong and are needed. Keegan would tell his psychologist that he didn't feel like he was loved despite being showered with it. What we learned was that he wasn't getting the type of affection he wanted. Even though he is 11 years old, he was jealous of the type of affection that his six-year-old brother and three-year-old nephew were getting from us. Even though we love everyone the same, we did have to realize that yes, a six-year-old and a three-year-old do receive a different kind of affection. We told Keegan that it had nothing to do with him, but it had more to do with their age and size. It is like him lying in bed or on the couch with us watching a movie while the babies (the six- and three-year-olds) were lying on our laps. The main struggle that we still have with Keegan is the meltdowns. It is so hard to watch him go through these and see the toll they take on him. I'm not saying I get it more than Michele, but I think I empathize with him more because I have walked where he is walking now. It is also very hard to watch the toll it is taking on Michele. We just started homeschooling this week, and she has already said that this will be the last year she is going to do it. This time, I really believe her. I don't think it will be the last year to homeschool Keegan but probably for Ian and Kai. I think it might be better if I could be at home more to help or had a job with hours that were more conducive to helping her out.

(I had to take a few days off from writing due to the news of the California pastor who took his own life. Hearing this and other stories like his hit me very hard. I just had to spend time praying for his family and for his church family. Also praying for all of us who live daily with depression and anxiety and for the ones who love us—especially, when we make it hard for them to love us. We all need to be praying that the stigma will be removed from all mental health issues so that we can have healthy, open dialogue with one another. There is no shame; we are not different or abnormal, and we need to be heard and not feel inadequate. I'm not saying this young man was not able to speak openly about his depression and anxiety; I am speaking for myself here. I know that inside most churches, such issues are not openly discussed as they can be seen as a "sin" problem—we aren't praying enough, or we are doing something wrong, and that is why we have this affliction in our life. I just pray for the day that the stigma is gone from all arenas and forums; that way people can get the healing that they need without fear or shame.)

Back to my Keegan update. We just got home from Keegan's psychologist appointment and unfortunately, there were more disclosures. We almost did not get to bring him home. They put us on a "safety plan," and we had to promise to keep a 24-hour watch on him. Not because he is a harm to himself, but because he disclosed that he was a harm to others. Keegan stated that he wanted 100 percent of both Michele's and my attention and affection and was willing to hurt and kill his little brothers to get it. As a parent, how do you process this information? Michele just sat there and cried as the psychologist was trying to clarify with Keegan that this is actually what he meant. The more he talked and asked questions, the more Keegan became upset, and I had to intercede to calm him down. I just used a calming tone and told him that it was going to be okay, and at first that seemed to make Keegan even madder, but then his anger turned to tears, and he balled up into the fetal position on the couch in this tiny office. I told Keegan to be careful with what he was saying, as both the doctor and I are mandated reporters, so he really needs to be aware of what he is saying. Keegan said that he loves his brothers, but he also wants to be the only child. Sadly, he didn't change his story and stuck by it, even yelling it at times. We just hugged him, said we loved him, and reassured him that we aren't giving up on him or his future.

Shortly after this latest revelation, we moved from Killeen down to the Austin area for Keegan's ongoing treatment needs, and we're hoping that this area will provide a nice change for Michele. Something that I haven't spoken much about is Michele and what she has been struggling with because I want her to write a book of her own. Her story is one that is truly heartbreaking for all that she has been through. But she suffers from severe agoraphobia and anxiety. There are a lot of days when she doesn't even leave our bedroom let alone the house. So, homeschooling wasn't going so well, and I had to make a decision that I really didn't want to make. I knew I was going to hurt Michele's feelings, but the kids were falling behind because they weren't doing any work because if they started acting up, it would cause her to have a panic attack. Once the attack happened, Michele would have to retreat to our room or take some medication; therefore, no schooling would get done.

I had to decide what to do. Should I send them all to school? Or send Ian and Kai to school but leave Keegan at home? So, I checked into the school that the kids would be attending and learned that it was an incredible school. And Keegan really wanted to go back to school, and he kept crying about how badly he wanted friends. We decided to send them back, but we held Keegan back in the fifth grade instead of putting him in the sixth grade as we felt that would be too much for him. So, the first week, we had a meeting with the teachers, and they were just incredible, and everything seemed great. Ian and Kai were doing wonderfully; Keegan claimed that he was happy, and all seemed well. Then Keegan wet his pants not once but twice in two weeks because he couldn't get his button undone fast enough, and it didn't help that he waited too long to go to the bathroom. To make things worse, Keegan went back to the classroom with his wet pants, and all his classmates saw him because he didn't know what to do or how to handle the situation, so kids made fun of him. Then, we learned that things hadn't been as great as Keegan had been saying. Keegan had been tattling on everyone or yelling at people when they were too loud and distracting him, or he sought justice when he thought it wasn't served. Long story short, the teachers told us that Keegan had alienated himself from the rest of his class due to his behavior. They tried to talk to him about choices and how to let things slide, but Keegan is just so "black and white," which is another similarity with myself.

The school has put him on a 504 plan and will be testing him soon, so they can offer more strategies that will help him to be able to cope. Sadly, his meltdowns have been increasing again, and his psychologist suggested that maybe it is because Keegan is internalizing all the stress of the day at school and then when he gets home, he just unloads. This is very possible because after one of his recent meltdowns, he cried to me saying he wanted to quit school. When I heard this, I knew this was going to be serious. Keegan started unloading all his feelings and hurts, and it was another heartbreaking memory for Michele and me. Keegan said that he had been lying to everyone at school to get kids to like him because no one likes him; he has no friends, and kids bully him. You know as a parent this is hard to hear, but it's worse when it's exactly the same struggle that I had. I just held him, told him that I loved him, and I said that the easy way out would be to let him quit and be homeschooled again, but that wouldn't help him. He knew that I was right, and he asked for our help. Keegan said, "Dad, I just want to be normal like everyone else." I told him that he is normal, that there isn't anything wrong with him. We sat there and talked with him about all the great things that make him awesome, and we told him that he doesn't have to lie or make things up about himself for people to like him. I said, "Keegan I know what it's like to feel different, but everyone at your age feels the same way. You just have to be Keegan; be yourself." He liked that, and Michele told him that even as adults we all still struggle with similar feelings and that people just want to fit in and be liked. He was amazed that adults have the same issues as kids.

There was something else we noticed about Keegan during this time. He was sleeping in our room during some of his meltdowns, and we noticed that he was snoring a lot and that he even paused or stopped breathing at times. Keegan's doctor referred him to a sleep doctor, and they sent him for a sleep study. During the sleep study, Keegan stopped breathing an average of 20 to 22 times an hour. He was diagnosed with severe sleep apnea. So, here we have a child with all these issues and to top it all off, he hasn't been getting a good night's sleep in who knows how long. Keegan got a CPAP machine, but we found out he wasn't using it; he takes it off when we leave the room, so he still isn't getting a good night's sleep. With the help of his psychologist, we worked on a reward system to get him to wear it. It's funny because Keegan will admit that he gets a great night of sleep when he wears it, but he says that it is annoying. The second part of the sleep apnea diagnosis was having him see an ENT specialist, and after meeting with him, it was determined that Keegan needed his tonsils and adenoids removed. A week later, he had them successfully removed, and he is still recovering. Just like his daddy, he's milking it for all its worth. I'm praying that the surgery will help with the sleep apnea or even cure it because going without sleep really plays havoc on a person.

Our oldest son Greyson is doing well; he didn't move out to Texas with us. He is at the age where he wants to be independent; we were so worried for him, but he is doing great. We have a lot of friends and my brother who live near him, so if he needs anything, there are plenty of people he can get help from in a pinch. He has always refused to talk about any diagnoses aside from ADHD, but this year he brought it up. Greyson told us that he has a friend and they were talking, and his friend joked that maybe Greyson has Asperger's or something. Greyson then said that after that and hearing about Keegan, it has made him think about things a lot. A few years ago, Greyson opened up about struggling with depression and suicide ideations, but he never told us till after he had graduated high school and refused to go get help. No, I take that back, he went to counseling one time and refused to talk to the counselor; he sat there for the whole hour and didn't talk.

(As I'm typing, I can hear Keegan screaming about something isn't fair.)

I'm back; it's going to be a long night I am thinking. But what else can you do for your kids? You pray for them, you love on them, but sometimes, our wiring, our chemistry is the way it is and, in my case and in my kid's case, it is genetics. It's like I know it isn't my fault, but it's hard not to blame myself. I love my kids so much, and I don't want them to hurt like I have; I want them to have a better life than I had.

I haven't spoken very much about our youngest, Kai, the six-year-old. We are watching him closely for any signs or cues. Is that normal? I mean I hate the fact that we "watch" our kids for possible signs of something, anything instead of just enjoying them. This has changed us so much, and now we just want to help others going through this, as it can be a very hard journey. But it is also a beautiful journey because every child is amazing, and it is our job as parents to reassure them that there is no "normal" and that they are fine the way they are. I mention Kai because he has a love for order; everything has to be in order, and he will get frustrated when it's not. He does not like loud noises and fixates or likes one thing at a time and sticks with that. But he is highly social and verbal, so maybe it's nothing, and we are just hypersensitive.

Ian, our 10-year-old, was diagnosed with mild ADHD; that is all we think he struggles with. He is shy but does not show any other signs like his brothers Keegan or Greyson. Ian does suffer the most from Keegan's abuses, and we try to buffer most of it as best we can. Honestly, we never know when Keegan will lash out or who he will lash out at. Kamron, our three-year-old grandson, does not have my genetics, but that does not mean he is in the clear. Kamron shows more symptoms than any of the children; he has a sensitivity to light and loud noises; he is very particular with food; and has a lot of social cues especially dealing with emotions. We are praying that if his dad gets him tested, he will be fine. I hate that I have possibly passed this on to my children. Oddly enough, one thing I have that no one else has is a super sensitive nose. I can smell things miles away before anyone else. I can also discern smells that others cannot; it is so strange. One bad thing that all of us share is very good hearing! Even whispers don't get by us! It can be annoying, trust me.

Playing in the background this morning as I type on the porch is MercyMe's "I Can Only Imagine," and I am imagining a future that is smooth. Just smooth and easy for a little bit, ha-ha. How about one smooth month? Last night for instance, we learned that Keegan, before he made this disclosure about hurting his brothers, took some shoelaces and tied them together and placed them around Ian's neck and hurt him. We weren't home, and no one told us until last night. Communication is vital in any relationship, but when dealing with children with diagnoses, it is crucial that everyone be on the same page on everything and communicating with one another. One thing that we have found out with Keegan is that he ran the house, and he knew it. Meaning that he learned that he could use his meltdowns to manipulate everyone to get what he wanted and to control each and every one of us. Through counseling and therapy, we have learned to take the control back from him by saying no. I know that sounds simple, but it's really not simple at all. You have to stand your ground and not budge from it, no matter what is thrown your way, until the storm subsides. What is hard for us is that we also have my parents living with us and you know grandparents; they don't want to see their grandkids crying and in pain. So, it has been tough to get everyone on the same page with this one because Keegan will manipulate like the best of them. It's like high-functioning kids or adults sometimes (and I speak from experience) will not always use their intelligence for good. Because as we all know the Dark Side has cookies, and those cookies are fun and exciting! It's a challenge and it's one that you have to wake up to every day and realize that it is for the best and your kid will still love you; saying no will not kill them or make you a bad parent.

Discipline

Spare the rod, spoil the child! Oh boy, you will learn quickly that with autism, ASD, ADHD, and any other disorder, you CANNOT discipline that disorder out of your child. You cannot spank them enough or hard enough, so just STOP!

Am I an expert? Actually, the states of Florida and Texas say that I am! Ha-ha. That is, I am an expert when I am testifying in court as a representative for Child Protective Services, anyway.

I will just tell you what we do, what we have learned along the way. These techniques work well with Keegan and all the kids. They also work well with other children, even extremely hyper children. I actually love taking hyper children and doing things in front of their parents to show them that there are better ways, or should I say, other ways. Say, for example, that a child did something wrong and I wanted to discipline them; this is what I would do with them. First, if the child is crying hysterically, they need to go calm down.

Keegan, like a lot of autistic kids, has a soother or box with items in it that help calm him down. He likes those fidget spinners. Some kids rub things on their faces, color, or a host of other things. Once they get to where they aren't hysterical, I get on their level. If it's a small child lying on the floor, I would lie on the floor and get eye to eye with them. Eye-to-eye contact is good; with some autistic children, that isn't always easy, but you try. You talk to them calmly (not yelling) and explain to them what they did wrong. Then, you explain to them that we don't do this and that; there will be consequences. Then, I have them repeat back to me what I said. If your child isn't verbal, you know when they understand or not. We write rules down and their consequences, so we can point them out. That way, no one can say, "That's not a rule . . . " or any nonsense like that. See, autistic children and ADHD children tend to be more concrete thinkers, so having things in writing will help them.

But also have a "cool off" spot in the house where they can go when they are having meltdowns or are hysterical and can't have that talk with you yet. The cool thing is, you will find like us, that Keegan will put himself in his cool off spot. He will say, "I am going to cool off" or "I need to cool off" and he will just go to his room and come out when he is ready.

This technique works with teenagers and adults too. Seriously, think about it, law enforcement and other authority figures use this technique all the time. Getting people to repeat things back to you shows that they at least heard you. In the CPS world, we do it with every instruction because parents are always trying to say, "You never told us this or that." "Yes, I told you if you smoke meth in the car with your child in it, that I was going to remove them." Children want to be heard, just like adults. Listen to them; let them talk to you and hear them out. It doesn't mean it's going to sway you or change anything, but it will make them feel that you are respecting them. That is a great feeling, agreed?

I mean, just because your kid has diagnoses doesn't mean you don't discipline them! Do not give in to them or let them use their diagnoses as a crutch! For Michele, that was her hang-up; she didn't want to be a "bad mom" or "mean mom." When a child claims that you don't love them and were mean or whatever hurtful statement they may make, please remember that you are doing great; they love you, and the tears will pass. God has beautiful plans for you, your child, and your family. Have faith and stay the course.

If you have questions about autism, ASD, or any other disorder, a lot of great resources are available. But the one great resource is a doctor! Also, I must stress the importance of finding a psychologist or even psychiatrist if there is a need for prescriptions.

So, as our time together comes to an end, I just want to thank you for stopping by! Check out my author pages on Facebook and Instagram, so we can chat, stay in touch, and connect!

But most importantly if your child, grandchild, or you have made comments about suicide, withdrawn from family and friends, or is suddenly overly happy and attached to the family, inquire, ask questions. A little known fact is that people who commit suicide are very happy before they take their life; they may show no noticeable signs of depression and make amends with loved ones. It is easier to ask someone how they are doing than to live with regrets that you didn't ask.

www.ingramcontent.com/pod-product-compliance
Lightning Source LLC
Chambersburg PA
CBHW030839090426
42737CB00009B/1029